P.4

THE RAILWAY SPIRIT

Train Life in Whisky Country

By R. I. SMITH

ACKNOWLEDGEMENTS

WRITING this book for the Keith and Dufftown Railway Association has been a wonderful experience. So many people have helped, and with more time it could be much longer as more and more railway workers past and present relate their experiences with such enthusiasm and pleasure in times shared and adventures enjoyed. My thanks go to so many people, including Jock Hay, the late Jim Keir, Hilda Duncan, Isobel Rugg, the late Isobel Sherrat, Ian Hird, Graham Maxtone, Keith Jones, Christine Robinson, Derek Pyper, Maureen Webster, chairman of the Keith and Dufftown Railway Association who had the idea in the first place, and, of course, my wife, Christine.

Ron Smith, Keith, May 2002

SOME of the illustrations in this book are not of the best quality of reproduction due to the ravages of time on the originals. The historical importance of these pictures is such that it was decided to include them anyway.

ISBN: 0-901845-22-1

The Keith & Dufftown Railway gratefully acknowledge the financial support received from Moray Council and Moray, Badenoch and Strathspey Enterprise

CONTENTS

FOREWORD

IT IS often said that the spectator sees most of the game and that is certainly true of Ron Smith.

A successful businessman, he has already chronicled his attempts to boost railways' fortunes in his excellent *Rail Freight in Moray* where he was frustrated at every turn by a combination of an inefficient and closure-minded management and bloody-minded trade unions.

Ron could have been forgiven for walking away from rail after his disheartening experience, but not a bit of it. His enthusiasm remains undimmed and here he takes us back to the halcyon days when Keith was a major rail centre and Speyside resounded to the healthy blast of the *Gordon Highlander* and her contemporaries.

He also highlights the men's slightly illegal methods of laying hands on a drop of the cratur, while at the same time giving a valuable insight into the workings of his beloved steam and paraffin oil railway.

Enthusiast or not, this is a book to savour and enjoy – I certainly did.

Jimmy Brown.

INTRODUCTION

IN THE North East of Scotland whisky and railways are inextricably intertwined. This area produces the majority of the world's best and purest malt whiskies, that are appreciated by connoisseurs the world over. Whisky of such distinction is made here because the water is uniquely soft and fresh, with a hint of peat, and the skills and knowledge to produce the amber nectar have been passed down the generations.

As the fame of whisky spread, and production increased, a brake on expansion came from the difficulty of transporting it to the markets in the south. Casks would be locally made, filled, and after maturity they would be strapped onto the backs of ponies for the long journey over the mountains. This was a very risky undertaking, as the precious cargo was the target of bandits and thieves. Before the advent of the railways, whisky was shipped in casks by coastal sailing ships to Edinburgh, London, Liverpool and elsewhere, for the local merchants to dilute or adulterate it as they wished, and then put into their own bottles for sale.

One of the great supporters and promoters of railways was Captain Grant of Elgin. He was a banker, and had built the Glen Grant Distillery at Rothes, and it produced (as it still does) an excellent malt. It went by horse to Lossiemouth docks for shipment south. He could clearly see that rail offered a much smoother, more secure and faster form of transport and pushed hard to have a line built through the Glen of Rothes, via Elgin to the sea. The great men of vision who were carving out the structure of the Great North of Scotland Railway (GNSR) could also see the potential of this industry and needed little pushing. Apart from bulk whisky, there was also the wood and iron for making casks, yeast, malted barley, and spent barley (draff) which with the benefit of rail could be sold for animal feed far away for the first time, coal for the boilers, parcels and machinery.

Connection or proximity to the railway became almost as important as proximity to a spring of suitable soft, pure water. Connecting lines were added to the GNSR, ranging from a simple spur at Strathmill Distillery, Keith, to the long line at Cromdale which branched off, followed the river under the A95 road, and off to Balmenach Distillery. The Strathmill spur was worked by the shunter from Keith Junction, which within living memory was a 24 hours a day 'turn'. Cromdale had its own shunting engine, or 'Puggie' as these locomotives were universally known in the North East, to work the traffic to and from the GNSR and shunt internally at the distillery.

In the days before 'just in time', the whisky train would amble down Speyside, shunting at so many places. Transporting whisky has always had its excitements and many are the tales of tampered bungs, sprung hoops, leaking staves, and even brace and bit holes up through the wooden floor of a van and through the bottom of a cask in order to obtain some illicit whisky away from the eyes of the ever-present 'Excise' who had to ensure that every penny of duty was guarded for the reigning monarch.

The close links between whisky distilleries and railways are continued today. The Keith and Dufftown Railway (KDR) links two prestigious distilleries, Glenfiddich at Dufftown and Strathisla at Keith. Their support is appreciated. Other links can be seen in the 'Wee Mac' diesel shunter which advertises Macallan whisky, the sponsors of its overhaul, and J & B who donated a large 0-6-0 diesel shunter. These locomotives have been of inestimable use on works trains supporting the back-breaking task of the volunteers who have laboriously cleared the line of decades of neglect to allow the superb re-launch of trains on the spectacular Keith to Dufftown railway line. This has brought back to life this portion of the GNSR which faithfully served the distilleries, and all the people who worked in the industry, for generations.

It was in 1845 that an Act of Parliament approved and allowed the construction of a railway from Aberdeen to Perth, to connect with the rapidly expanding network of railways in Britain. This coincided with a demand to link Inverness with the south, and initially, it was planned to achieve this by running along the Moray Firth and through Aberdeen. However, by the time that the plan reached Parliament the Invernesians were promoting a direct line over the mountains to Perth. This did not prevent Parliament approving the Bill to construct the Great North Of Scotland Railway in 1846, and by joining up with other railways, linking the two important towns. The first sod was cut at Westhall, Aberdeen on November 25, 1852. The line was not difficult to build and was formally

Down passenger train beside Loch Park, Drumuir C. 1910 (GNSR).

opened to Huntly on September 19, 1854. The more difficult countryside to Keith was conquered with trains running through in 1856.

Meanwhile, Inverness was pressing ahead and as well as the direct line south, branched off at Forres to Elgin, and onwards to Keith to form the through route. This was finally achieved in 1858.

Meanwhile, another wee railway, the Morayshire Railway, had opened in 1852, connecting Elgin to the coast at Lossiemouth. The man behind this was Captain Grant, an Elgin banker who owned Glen Grant Distillery at Rothes, and was keen to transport his whisky to the ships that would take it to the lucrative southern markets. The arrival of the 'big railway' encouraged the Morayshire line to use part of the new railway and then branch off it to reach the heart of distillery country at Rothes and Craigellachie, which it completed in 1858.

Railway construction continued. The line from Keith to Dufftown opened on February 1, 1862. By 1863, another line ran from Dufftown to a junction at Craigellachie and on to Abernethy. This was further extended to Boat of Garten where it connected up with the Inverness to Perth line on August 1, 1866.

Other lines quickly followed to the coast, running from a junction called Cairnie on the Aberdeen side of Keith to a junction at Tillynaught where another, short, branch ran to Banff. The coast line continued along the spectacular single line round to Elgin, giving a choice of three routes between Keith and Elgin. Other branches went from the main line at Inverurie to Oldmeldrum, from Inveramsay to Macduff, Kintore to Alford, and Dyce to termini at Boddam, Peterhead and Fraserburgh. One other line completed the GNSR system, from Aberdeen to Ballater. The GNSR certainly had its eye on the distillery traffic when it extended the network up Strathspey towards Aviemore, but the arrival of the line had a greater effect than anticipated. Now whisky could quickly, easily and cheaply be transported to the south markets. There was a growth in demand and new distilleries were needed to supply this lucrative marked. Proximity to the railway, as well as to a good source of water, became the criteria for finding suitable locations.

Aberlour, Balmenach and Carron (Daluaine) were served by horse and cart. Craggenmore was the first distillery to be built after the line opened. The distillery opened in 1869 and was conveniently sited near Ballindalloch Station. This was the start of a veritable boom. Aberlour was enlarged and rebuilt to the present site in 1879; Aultmore, near Keith, opened in 1897; Balvenie at Dufftown in 1892; Benriach towards Elgin in 1898; Benromach at Forres in 1898; Caperdronich at Rothes in 1897; Cardow in 1884; Coleburn 1896; Convalmore 1894; Craigellachie 1890; Dallas Dhu 1899; Dufftown 1896; Glendullan 1897; Glen Elgin 1899; Glenfiddich 1887; Glenlossie 1876; Glen Moray 1897; Glenrothes 1878; Glen Spey 1885; Glentauchers 1898; Imperial 1897; Inchgower at Buckie 1871; Knockando 1898; Knockdhu 1894; Langmorn 1895; Macallan

1886; Speyburn at Rothes 1897; Strathmill, Keith 1891; Tamdhu 1896.

This prodigious rate of construction did result in over-production. At the turn of the century there were cutbacks and a few distilleries were closed and mothballed, indeed Benriach was closed in 1900 and Caperdonich in 1901 and neither reopened until the 1960s.

All this surge in production created very welcome traffic flows for the railway.

The first whisky special was recorded in 1887 when 16,000 gallons of malt whisky from Craggenmore were dispatched from Ballindalloch in a special train destined for merchants in Dundee. Other occasional bulk movements created surges in traffic. In 1922 Craigellachie Distillery must have been short of maturation space as it despatched 120,000 gallons to Campbelltown Distillery for warehousing. This involved special trains running through to Lossiemouth. Here the whisky was transhipped into two steam coasters who took it round the North of Scotland to the Mull of Kintyre.

This special industry influenced the character of the region and particularly the railway traffic. The people working on the railway knew the importance of the traffic and worked hard to ensure that the essential service was provided all the year round. This book tells some of the day-to-day stories of working the whisky, and other, trains in this unique part of Scotland.

WHISKY TRAINS OPERATIONS

THE close co-operation between the whisky and the railway industries was born of a mutual dependence and respect. The local railwaymen certainly understood the needs and nature of the whisky industry that supported the employment of the local area's inhabitants – sometimes they understood it too well!

It is still possible for an individual to purchase whisky straight from the still. It is then stored in a bonded warehouse (meaning that duty has not yet been paid) in an oak cask for a specified number of years. It is then delivered to the customer either in the cask, or specially bottled. One Friday morning, a small cask known as a firkin, which holds about nine gallons, was at Boat of Garten for onward delivery to a Mr William

Crew taking the guard back with them as they leave Boat of Garten shed to back down onto the train.

Whitelaw at Knockando House Halt. This was obviously a special cask of whisky, it must have been a very mature single malt. The Halt was a private platform just for the big house and was not in the public timetable. The name Whitelaw was significant, one Mr Whitelaw was a director of the London & North Eastern Railway, which had absorbed the Great North, and an A4 Pacific streamlined express steam locomotive, had been named 'William Whitelaw' after him. It would be foolish to just deposit the firkin onto the platform and depart – it would very quickly disappear. It was arranged that the cask would be safely locked away in Boat station and delivered on the Monday passenger train when someone would meet it at the Halt.

On the Monday the crew went in to pick up the precious cask, and found it empty. This was a high-profile crime, a special, very desirable malt whisky had disappeared, and incidentally, it was consigned to a special dignitary. The railway detective was sent for. He was universally known as Dick Barton after the popular special agent character on the radio. Everyone concerned was summoned to be interviewed in the investigation. Dick Barton was completely lost as to how the whisky had been removed from the cask. There was no sign of tampering. No matter how closely he examined the cask he could not find a clue. Just to 'get one over' on Dick Barton, to show superior knowledge, one railwayman said

Shunter Charlie Mitchell (Keith) finds a bird's nest on wagon solebar.

that he could show how it could be done. Dick Barton was sceptical.

The railwayman picked up a metal bar that was part of the parcel-weighing machine and carefully tapped around the cask. From the sound, he could tell that a hoop had been loosened. He tapped it gently off the cask, revealing a neatly bunged drill hole, with another exactly opposite it on the other side of the cask. The hoop had been removed, the whisky poured out into a suitable container, the holes filled up with spiles of wood, and the hoop chapped back into place. If the cask were to be filled with water, no leak would be found. The detective was flabbergasted. He never did discover who had taken the whisky, but from then on he always kept a careful watch on that railwayman – he knew too much about the ways of making whisky disappear!

Whisky always was, and still is, a form of currency, and is often used as a 'thank you'. During one winter of heavy snow, the Speyside goods locomotive was working with the small snow plough on the front buffer beam, just to keep the line clear as it worked up to Aviemore, shunting at all the sidings on the way. At Tamdhu Distillery, one of the stillmen asked if the crew would clear the tracks into the still, and then shunt in a couple of open wagons that were waiting there to be loaded with full casks to be taken south. This would allow the still to use the wagons to dump their draff into them, as the roads were blocked and the lorries couldn't get in to them. Otherwise they would have to close down production. Draff is the wet barley after it has been used to make the whisky. It is used as animal feed by farmers all over Scotland. The loco men happily obliged, and when they had finished their manoeuvres, the stillman appeared again with a healthy great dram for each of the crew, driver, fireman and guard.

Sometimes the temptation of being so close to so much whisky proved irresistible. A well known and specialised grocers in Elgin, Gordon & McPhail, produce a full range of whiskies, including their own label brands. They buy whisky at the still and pay for storage, calling in casks from all over Scotland, usually a few from each distillery to make up their limited edition bottlings. One day, the pick-up goods was booked to call at Ballindalloch to collect two open wagons with casks for Gordon & McPhail. These could easily be less than full wagon loads, and so the casks would be roped carefully into place on their ends. By their shape, casks are not easy to rope, and it was a specialised knack, well known by the railwaymen.

On arriving at Ballindalloch, there was no sign of the signalman. Being well used to operating the system, the crew assumed that they must just be short staffed that day and no-one had told them, so they set about their work. The fireman operated the signals and points, and the locomotive shunted into the shed 'road'. This shed was locked, but the crew knew where the key was always hidden, unlocked the shed, opened the big doors and eased the loco in to couple onto the two wagons. Even over the

40650 leaves Ballindalloch heading south with an officers special.

steam, smoke and hot oil smell of the locomotive the driver could strongly smell whisky. He shouted to the fireman who was walking up onto the loading bank that one of the casks must be a 'leaker' and to have a look into the wagons. What he saw surprised even a Speyside man. One of the casks had been drilled and was still weeping whisky. The floor of the wagon was soaking, and lying flat out, dead drunk, was the signalman. He must have been drinking straight from the cask after he had drilled it, unable to resist the fine mature whisky.

With a fine sense of priorities the driver hammered a spile into the drill hole. Then the spile was liberally clarted in soot and dirt to hide the evidence. Hopefully, when the wagon arrived in Elgin the Excise man would assume that it was a leaker, the whisky lost was on the wagon floor, and no duty would have to be paid. If any at all was suspected of being consumed, the full duty would have to be paid. The actual cost of the whisky would be around £9 per gallon, but the duty would be around £86 per gallon. Plus, it would mean an investigation. Now, with the help of the guard, they lifted the signalman out onto the loading bank. Not feeling any sympathy or charity for him, he was dragged along on his bottom to the engine and deposited onto the running plate under the smokebox. The wagons were pulled out, the shed locked and the key put back in the hiding place. Then the loco pulled up alongside the signal box. The crew once again manhandled the inert signalman, up the stairs into the box and left him lying there. They then reformed the train, operated the signals and points, and continued the trip. At the next station the signalman came over and asked why they had been so long at Ballindalloch, and was anything wrong there as he couldn't raise the signalman on the telephone. The crew explained the situation, they had secured the signals, operated the single line tablet apparatus, and everything was in order. The signalman was happy and carried on.

The next day the same crew was again working the whisky train. The signalman at Ballindalloch was bright and cheerful – no sign of his previous day's excesses, and he carried on as normal. Eventually, the signalman was caught red-handed at Carron. Dick Barton was up in a tree with binoculars and a camera and caught the signalman crouching in a wagon drilling into a cask. He was instantly dismissed.

The camaraderie and co-operation of railwaymen and stillmen certainly ensured that things were done and progress made without officialdom necessarily knowing. As they were shunting wagons at Knockando the men managed to de-rail a wagon. Rather than call Control and delay things while engineers were called, the men decided to sort it themselves. Lying in the yard were a couple of wedges. These devices were not to be used anymore, as they were dangerous. However, the crew knew how to use them. The wagon was pulled up the wedge and dropped obligingly back onto the rails. Authority would never know. Unfortunately, the frog of the point was damaged in the process, and this would have to be reported, as it would need repair. This now entailed an inquiry and a report. The inspector arrived and assembled the culprits.

When he saw the staff who had been involved, he knew that he would never obtain the correct story from them. The inspector sighed, he would never find out the exact truth. He listened to the story that they had decided to tell him, wrote it down, and filed the report.

The distilleries traffic included yeast, a vital ingredient in the distilling process. Yeast is a living organism and requires air to breathe and

LNER 62271 at Blacksboat Station going from Craigellachie to Aviemore 1950s.

preferably a temperature of around +3C° It is produced at specific yeast plants, or is brought from beer breweries. Yeast was regular traffic and was carried in either wooden barrels or hessian sacks. In hot weather the yeast would multiply and ooze out of the bags. These were sewn across the top creating two screwed up 'ears' to lift them by, each bag weighed about half-a-hundred weight (56lb. or 25kg.) and small quantities would be carried in the guard's van compartment on the passenger train. The yeast would spread all over the floor, making a slippery mess with a very strong, but not unpleasant, smell. Manhandling the bags in the summer left men with their hands and overalls liberally covered in yeast. A 'van fit' (a 12-ton capacity two-axle vacuum braked van) was always on the 12.17 goods train from Perth which arrived in Forres around 16.20, with yeast for the local distilleries. The bags of yeast were given priority and swiftly loaded onto the railway lorry, a Scammell three-wheel tractor unit and single-axle flat trailer, for delivery to Glenburgie, Ben Romach and Dallas Dhu distilleries. This enthusiasm to ensure prompt delivery was possibly connected with the dram that the lorry driver received at each still. A late delivery could result in delivering after the stillmen had gone off shift and no dram would be forthcoming.

At Boat of Garten extra sidings had been laid to cope with all the distillery traffic. The goods train from the south would shunt traffic here into groups of wagons in the order they needed to be for delivery along

61347 calls at Drummuir with the 1425 Aberdeen-Elgin on 3/6/60.

the route to Keith. This shunting took place in the loop, while the passenger train used the through line platform. Once the passenger train had set off north, that line could be used as well. However, this was once used a little too soon and a van wagon of yeast briskly shunted into the through road and off it sailed after the passenger train, unnoticed by the busy railwaymen. Farther along the line a farmer's wife spotted the van trundling along and rang Boat of Garten to ask if they had lost a wagon. After a bit of checking, they admitted that a wagon was missing and the loco was sent off after it. The next day the goods were shunted, the Speyside train made up and departed. Later, a phone call was received at Boat of Garten asking where the yeast van was. This was assumed to be a leg-pull, but the distillery insisted that the yeast van had not arrived in their siding and where was it? Phone calls were made up and down the lines but there was no trace of it. Then a railwayman happened to ask why a van full of yeast was sitting on the turntable. It had been wrongly shunted, not noticed, and left where it had stopped right in the middle of the turntable.

Distilleries also used a lot of coal to fire the boilers and this produced steady traffic flows, as did coal to the town gas works in Keith. A horse and cart worked at this steadily every day and it is said that the driver was always so drunk that he slept on the cart, hunched on the seat. The old horse just plodded all the way to the gas works, then ambled back down, all by his own sense, with the driver fast asleep.

The arrangements for delivering the coal were all much the same. Ballindalloch was typical. The coal wagons were dropped off the goods train and shunted into the siding. The railwaymen would uncouple them one by one and manoeuvre them over the chute; this was done with the aid of a 'pinch bar'. This is a long pole with a round metal clad flat point at the end. This is jammed under the rear wheel and levered upwards and the wagon then rolls forward a little, the doors opened and the coal falls down the chute into the railway lorry below and the remaining coal shovelled out. The lorry then shuttled up and down to the various distilleries. The big lorry stationed there had a big LNER stencilled over the cab when that railway took over the Great North. This amused the locals who from then on called it the 'Liner'.

Invergordon Distillery was powered by heavy oil from the Bowling oil terminal on the River Clyde. Deliveries of this oil could not be delayed, it left the terminal at a warm temperature and would thicken to such a degree that it would not flow from the tank if left too cool. If this happened it had to be taken all the way back down to Bowling where there were steam pipes to bring the temperature up and make the liquid flow again and then the dash was on to get to Invergordon. During this time the distillery would be running low on fuel.

One delivery of oil tanks was shunted a little too roughly and on the curves one tank rode up over another, locking the buffers together. This caused problems and the carriage and wagon examiner was hurriedly called for to assess the situation and probably call for the re-railing vehicle from Inverness. The carriage and wagon examiner man was at Forres and responding to the urgent pleas from Invergordon, decided that the quickest way was to throw some tools into his own car and drive straight up there. When he arrived, he could see that there was no damage so he set about sorting it out, scorning the idea of calling the re-railing crew who were based in Inverness. By now it was dark, but with the feeble light cast over from the distillery he set about loosening the bolts that held the buffers on the wagon that was off the ground. He borrowed a couple of empty barrels and positioned them under the buffers. Then he removed the top pair of bolts and kept the bottom pair just hanging on the last thread. With a quick nudge they were out, the buffers were off and the wagon dropped neatly onto the rails. Now, using the barrels as a platform he lifted the hydraulic buffers up and slid the bolts in place. This required quite some strength and would certainly not confirm to modern health and safety regulations. He tightened up the bolts, checked round and returned the barrels. Little did he know that he had been observed.

He reported to the station that the wagons were no longer buffer-locked, no damage had been done and they were ready to be shunted in. On reporting for duty the next day, the Chief called him in to tell him that he had done a good job, but Invergordon had reported that he was 'not human'. The carriage and wagon man could not understand, he had been called a lot of things in his time, but never 'not human'. What were they saying? Invergordon had reported that the carriage and wagon man had been witnessed lifting the 16-ton tank wagon by himself, back on to the rails. This is how legends are made.

The distilleries produce two useful by-products – draff, which is the spent barley, and pot ale, this is a thick dark brown liquid, the residue from the copper pot stills after primary distillation has taken place. Pot ale is also used for animal feed as it is high in protein. It is about half the food value of sugar molasses but also about half the price. Some farmers like to pour it on to straw as an additive and the cattle like it. In order to add value to these by-products and make them easier to store and transport over greater distances, plants were built to dry the draff, combine it with the pot ale and make pellets. Rothes has many distilleries, Caperdonich, Glenspey, Glen Grant, Glenrothes, and Speyburn just up the glen to Elgin, and the companies joined together to fund the construction of a big plant called 'The Combination of Rothes Distillers Purification Works' or, as it was commonly known 'The Purie'. This was rail connected but the product mostly went by road as it degraded with handling into and out of rail wagons.

Invergordon was not part of 'The Purie', having their own plant for this production, and a trial was made with special 'Presflo' wagons to try to capture this traffic. Presflo wagons were built specifically for cement powder, which is difficult material to handle. It has a steep 'angle of repose' which means that it does not flow very well. The Presflo wagons were fitted with pipes to enable them to be connected to a shore air supply and the air would mix with the cement and blow it out into silos. The theory of using these wagons was good, but in practice it was found that the carrying capacity of the wagons was fine for a heavy commodity like cement, but relatively little for a light bulky material like the dark grains

78054 at Craigellachie with the 10.20am to Boat of Garten.

pellets. Despite treading it down and packing it in as much as possible, no economical quantity could be loaded into a wagon in order to make the rate per ton viable, and the traffic remained on the road.

The typical GNSR goods shed on the line was made of overlapping wooden planks, rather like a clinker built boat. At Craigellachie the goods shed was easily accessible from a road, and two 'worthies' decided to help themselves to some whisky. During the night they crept down to the shed and prised off two planks at ground level. They squeezed through underneath the loading platform, which was also constructed of wood,

Standard Class 2 2-6-0 78053 with two-coach train for the Speyside line at Craigellachie.

with stout timbers as befits a loading platform. The two men set to work with a brace and bit and bored up through the floor. Then they continued to drill right up into the bottom of a whisky cask. The whisky came pouring out, and enough was collected to satisfy their needs. They tried to push a spile up into the bottom of the cask to plug it. Then, hopefully, the loss would not be noticed. However, they had not thought about the lip of the cask. There was a gap between the end of the cask and the floor, and they just could not manage to push the spile up. Each time it poked up above the floor, the flow of whisky washed it away. After several attempts, no doubt with whisky flowing liberally down their arms, they gave up and made their escape, leaving the cask to drain away all over the floor and down their hole.

Some distilleries were content to let the railway or a local carter, collect and deliver from the nearest station the multiplicity of goods ranging from coal, yeast and grain to machinery, casks and stationery. Others had their own sidings, such as Tamdhu and Knockando, both leading from Knockando Station, and Imperial at Carron. Others had their own lines and locomotives. By 1885 Daluaine and Balmenach both had their own lines with their own locomotives, invariably known as 'puggies'. Latterly, Daluaine had a 1939 Andrew Barclay 0-4-0 saddle tank which has survived and is now at Aberfeldy Distillery. The Balmenach puggie had quite a run from the railway sidings at Cromdale up through the village and on to the distillery. The little tank engine was only fit to propel two coal wagons at a time and could be heard working hard practically all the way to the still, its frantic bark echoing across Strathspey.

Returning empty wagons to Cromdale was usually organised as one

Dailuine Distillery.

trip with up to eight empties forming a rake, with their brakes pinned down. One day the puggie set off and found out too late that no-one had pinned the brakes down. The wagons pushed the puggie which shot down towards Cromdale, through the gate that usually was closed against the siding, derailed and ended up in a field. Fortunately, no one was hurt.

When the line from Keith to Aviemore was closed, the railway wanted to keep the whisky traffic and efforts were made to use it to feed into the remaining Inverness to Aberdeen line. Railway lorries brought the full casks to Elgin where they were manhandled into van wagons for the journey south. This was clearly not ideal as they had to be manhandled out again into lorries for final delivery at the other end. Road competition was, by now, unbeatable. More powerful lorries could run from a Speyside distillery to a bonded warehouse in Glasgow in half a day, compared to a three-day transit by train. An overhead gantry crane was installed at Elgin around 1969. Now containers could be used which avoided double handling. Unfortunately, this was not a success. The crane was built on a short length of track, straddling two sidings which curved. As the crane did not have differential bogies, it could not go round curves. This meant that the wagons would have to be moved under the crane by a shunting loco. At that time there was always a shunting loco on duty at Elgin to do this, but it destroyed part of the advantage of the crane. Due to politics, the service at the other end ran into Glasgow High Street where a temporary mobile crane was used. This was because Freightliner had been set up to handle all inter-modal traffic and this traffic did not fit into their plan so it was always operated by BR, and then Scotrail, using just a handful of unique wagons converted from other types. By now, the early 1970s, Health and Safety concerns were becoming more pressing and there had to be lights inside the containers. This was not difficult for a road lorry which had batteries but difficult to do in a container as there was nowhere to fix them. Portable lights were tried, but they were always being damaged or misplaced. Casks were rolled into a lorry or a container on the bilge and then up-ended. This is quite a task as the lightest would be around five hundredweight (250kg.) and the heaviest, around 11 hundredweights (550kg.) Then 8ft. x 4ft. boards were laid on top and another layer of casks rolled in and up-ended. With the road vehicle, the driver could keep an eye on the 'topping-boards' and put them back into his lorry. With the rail movement, the boards were always disappearing and this created yet another cost.

Probably the final nail in the coffin was the advent of the 'crown lock' van. This system meant that the casks would be loaded onto a lorry that had a unique 'CLV' number that indicated that it conformed to a specific type. A padlock and seal went on the door and this was not broken or opened until it reached the bonded premises at the destination. Accompanying it was a special book that detailed all the movements of the vehicle, complete with signatures. The distillery, therefore, did not have to pay duty on the whisky. It was difficult for the railway to keep a close watch on these details and lost books and padlocks caused lots of delays and rejections. With the rebuilding of the A9 into a First Class road, making the road journey much quicker and more reliable, resulting in better utilisation of equipment and lower cost, the railway finally lost the traffic, including the coal, grain, draff and yeast.

One company tried hard to continue with rail. Chivas Bros., bought the old loco depot at Keith and in the early 1970s built a blending plant on the site, incorporating one of the original loco shed walls into the new building. Malt whisky was tankered down from any of their eight distilleries to Keith and filled into casks for storage and maturation at the huge complexes at Malcolmburn and Keith. Then casks from the warehouses were taken to the new plant for emptying into the big vats to mix and form blended malts such as Chivas Regal. Then the bulk whisky passed via a loading gantry into demountable tanks on flat wagons. Twice a day the train ran to Glasgow where the tanks were shunted directly into Chivas premises and emptied for bottling. This worked well for years, even though the small fleet of flat wagons were old and non-standard conversions. The end came when anything other than full train load traffic was discouraged as being uneconomical. The 'trip' into the Chivas premises in Glasgow was discontinued on the pretext of saving a locomotive. The train now ran into Freightliner at Coatbridge who would lift the tanks off and drive them into Glasgow and back again empty. The goods train to Keith was reduced to one a day which tripled the transit time. Freightliner only had one crane that could lift from the bottom. The Chivas tanks were swap bodies which do not lift from the top like containers. When the Freightliner crane broke down, consistently spraying hydraulic oil over the tanks, no department of the railway would pay for the repair. High capacity road tanks could take 50% more per load, and be down and back in a day. The traffic was lost to road.

DRIVING THE ENGINES

THE whisky train was a slow affair by today's standards. It started shunting the first sidings at 8a.m., and the final trainload would be at Aviemore by 10p.m. for the night run over the 'Hill' (through the pass of Drumochter) and to the Glasgow whisky blending and bottling plants. The traffic was steady, with peaks on Tuesdays and Thursdays, when the train would be long and heavy. Anything less than a Black Five 4-6-0 would struggle.

In January 1953 there was a fierce storm which brought chaos to a lot of Britain, and brought down power lines, telephone lines, and a lot of trees onto the railway line. The whisky train was waiting for the first

Leaving Aberdeen for the South.

The 7.10 from Keith ran into falling trees at Drumuir on 31/1 1953.

passenger train to come into the loop, then they would set off up Speyside. Imagine their amusement when the D41 4-4-0 arrived festooned with telephone wires and bits of poles and trees – and without its chimney. The driver of the passenger train was quite philosophical about it, but it meant that the loco would not steam properly and so couldn't continue. It was during this storm that the wooden waiting room at Ballindalloch took off, smacked a guard on the side of his head as he walked forward to check on the delays, and then landed on the opposite platform. The signalman reported that as all communications were down, and the line probably blocked, Control had decided to suspend all trains meantime. When the line was reopened, there were a lot of trees to move, and long bogie bolster wagons were sent to the area to be left in various sidings for complete tree trunks to be loaded on and sent south.

This additional freight made the goods trains even heavier. While shunting at Ballindalloch, the crew were setting off when the second bogie bolster wagon derailed and started to run up the platform. The train crew quickly halted and the fireman asked what they should do. The driver reckoned that if they just reversed, the wagon might go back onto the rails again and no-one would know. This they cautiously did, and the wagon rejoined the rails. A quick examination revealed nothing wrong, and so they carefully set off again. Once again the cantankerous wagon left the rails and mounted the platform. The driver had had enough of this, he reversed once more and amazingly the wagon went docilely back onto the rails. They decided that they would detach the wagon, shunt it into the siding, and set off on their way. The signalman was not happy about this at all. Higher authority would have to be informed, carriage and wagon examiners sent for to check the wagon, and they were running over time and were in danger of delaying the passenger train – a cardinal sin and one that could incur the dreaded letter of reprimand. The crew told the signalman what they thought of him, and that they were not taking that wagon anywhere. They swiftly shunted it into the siding, reformed the goods train, and set off in fine style.

Working the whisky train demanded a high level of skill and co-operation from the crew. The weight of the train could vary a lot. Sometimes a distillery would have just three or four casks securely roped in a wagon, sometimes several full wagons. One night, after the last pick up, the train was loaded to 44 wagons plus a guard's van, and the engine was just a modestly powered Class D40 number 62271. The driver asked the fireman if they would 'stick' that night. Just the week before he had been transferred from Elgin depot and was not fully used to the route. The fireman remembered a fortnight before when, with a similar heavy train, on the rising bends before Cromdale the howling wind had brought the loco to its knees, with it only managing to turn the wheels slowly between gusts. The fireman considered, and predicted that they would stall at the bridge between Advie and Grantown. The driver took this as a challenge and instructed the fireman to keep a good head of steam on her and he would get her through. Setting off gradually to take up the slack in the

62271 GNOSR engine Class D40.

couplings, he then opened her up and off they stormed. Sure enough, they slowed, and slowed and finally stalled right under the bridge. With the full head of steam the safety valves blew off and dislodged the accumulated muck from the underside of the bridge and it showered down over the engine. The driver demanded to know how his mate had been able to so accurately predict where they would stall. The wagons were all 'loose coupled'. That means that they were not vacuum braked, and were joined by three link couplings. When going down a dip, the guard had to screw on his handbrake in his van to keep the couplings taut. Otherwise, when the train ascended the other side of the dip, the 'snatch'

Moving the coal forward.

Willie Loban and Jim Keir at the Boat of Garten in the 1950s.

on the couplings became progressively worse along the train until the force could break a coupling, splitting the train, and also jerk the guard off his feet or fling him around in his van. The fireman knew the guard that night, and he knew that he was not one to help the drivers by being light handed on the brake. The combination of the guard and the heavy train was enough to cause them to stall. As the driver had the single line token, no other train could enter that section, so they were quite safe.

They decided to split the train, take half to Grantown and return for the other half. Brakes were pinned down, precautions taken, and the train

LNER D40 and crew at Boat of Garten 1950s.

split. The guard was left in his van with half the wagons, and he stoked up the stove and settled down to wait. The crew set off with the first half of their train. At Grantown, the fireman went to the signal box to report. The signalman asked for the token. The fireman refused to give it up, saying that he needed it to go back for the rest of the wagons. The signalman insisted that he give up the token as he would otherwise be holding up the passenger train, and would receive a letter of reprimand. Again the fireman refused and the discussion became heated. The signalman rang Control and reported what was going on – he wasn't going to have a delayed passenger train blamed on him. Control asked to speak to the fireman and told him to give up the token, let the passenger train through, and then go back for the rest of the goods train, which was presumably shunted into the siding. The fireman explained that their wagons were on the running line, because the siding was full of condemned vans waiting to be taken away for scrapping, and he wasn't stupid. Confusion sorted out, Control authorised them to go and collect the wagons immediately. The fireman returned to his engine, and was then sent back to the signalbox again. The loco was running low on water after all this time, and the driver refused to go. The loco was detached from the passenger train (much to its crew's disgust as they would now be late home, missing a change-over) and the wagons retrieved.

On another stormy night, the heavily laden train reached '30-mile curve' before Boat of Garten and was struggling. The engine was a K2 2-6-0 and it was so cold that the injector froze. This meant that they could not inject water into the boiler to maintain steam, and this could end in a boiler explosion. The crew had no choice other than to halt the train and throw out the fire. The fireman ensured that there were a few embers carefully gathered at the rear of the firebox. The guard stoked up his stove and settled down for the night. The driver and fireman, keeping hold of the single line token, walked to the Boat through the snow. They told the signalman the position and went home to bed, still with the token. This ensured that no other train could enter the section and hit the goods train. Next morning, the crew returned by foot through the snow to the K2. The injector had thawed out. The embers were spread out from their corner and the fire coaxed into life. As soon as sufficient pressure was achieved, they set off for the Boat. All in a day's work for the hardy crews.

The K2s were foreign locos, being originally designed by the Great Northern Railway in England. The driver had to stand on the 'wrong' side of the footplate, which meant that he, rather than the fireman, would have to hand over the token to the signalmen. The token was carried in a leather pouch that was attached to a large bamboo hoop so that if needed, it could be scooped up by the outstretched arm of the signalman or fireman. One winter's day, the driver could not get the token out of the shiny new pouch with its stiff leather. In his frustration, he held it upside down and banged it on the cab side. The token shot out, rolled across the cab floor and out into the snow. This caused chaos, and it could not be found, despite hunting around in the snow for quite an area. Long after the snow had finally thawed and gone, the token was found some distance away from the lineside. It was presumed to have been carried away by the melting snow.

Another item lost overboard was a precious piece box (lunch box) One driver used a First World War mess tin as his piece box. These were specially shaped so that they did not cause chaffing when hung on a waist belt, and it had belonged to his father. On this particular day, he had been fishing early in the morning and had caught two prime salmon. He came from Forres and had a regular sale for his salmon at a high-class hotel

62713 LNER D49/1 'Aberdeenshire' at Hawick shed 1950s.

there. He was keen to get back to Forres to collect his money for the salmon. The crew was working north from Boat of Garten on the goods train, and was due to change over with the crew of the southbound goods at Knockando. On changing over they took charge of a K2. They agreed that the fireman would drive, as hard as he could, while the driver would fire hard to ensure a full head of steam. Then at the Boat, the driver could quickly jump off and catch the Forres direct train, leaving the fireman the job of disposing of the engine on the shed. This they did. The fireman thrashed the loco up towards the Boat. They had to dash from section to section to cross the passenger train higher up the line than usual. The passenger could not be delayed so they probably broke all records for a freight train on the line. No doubt if authority ever knew, they would think that they had a very dedicated crew. The K2s had a ledge at the front of the tender where the crew would put their things, including piece boxes. With the thrashing of the loco, the ride was rather lively, and the precious piece box slipped off the ledge, bounced across the footplate and out the doorway. The driver was inconsolable. He cursed the fireman all the way to the Boat – although he loudly protested his innocence. He was only driving in such a manner so that the driver could make the connection to Forres after all, and if the piece box was so precious why was he using it every day? Why not keep it safe at home? This grumbling continued all the way to the Boat, where the driver jumped down and crossed to the Forres train, which slowed to pick him up as he, of course, was known to the other driver, as all the men knew each other.

This left the fireman with the job of disposing of the engine, throwing out the remains of the fire and doing all the housekeeping that went with steam engines.

The following day the two men were on the same duty, and still the driver continually berated the fireman for losing his piece box for him. There was a load of grass seed to be delivered to Advie siding, so once backed into the siding, the crew set off along the track to look for the piece box. Alongside the River Spey were the tents of the travelling folk. They came every year at this time to fish for pearls. They had tin cans with glass in the bottoms to peer through the water for the fresh water oysters. There were piles of shells on the banks, from all the fruitless oysters that had been fished out. The practice is not allowed now, as the oysters are an endangered species. There was no control then, and the river was just plundered. The crew searched in vain, and in the end decided that the pearl fishers must have found it and would be taking it away to sell it. There was no point in asking them if they knew anything about it. They rejoined the engine, with the driver in a black mood. At the end of the shift the fireman lost his temper, there was a shouting match which cleared the air and it was never mentioned again.

The GNSR was famously described as having a great variety of loco-motive types – small 4-4-0s, medium 4-4-0s and large 4-4-0s. Only one has survived, number 49 'Gordon Highlander' (the Gordons came from GNSR territory) and is currently in Glasgow Museum. At one time she was allocated to Boat of Garten shed which was coded 60B under the BR scheme, and was a sub shed of Aviemore, which itself came under 60A Inverness. She was rostered to take the two coach Speyside passenger train to Keith. The crew prepared her, and as she was due to finish her 'turn' at Keith there was no need to fill the tender with coal. This would be left to the Keith men to do when they prepared her for the next duty. The fireman went into the tender to shovel the coal forward, while the driver would oil round and use the loading bank to reach the Westinghouse pump to lubricate it. This pump created the air pressure for the loco brakes. When it was time, they set off and backed down onto the coaches in the station platform. Imagine their consternation when they found that they had no brakes. The dials were obscured with dirt and the crew had not noticed that the air pressure was at zero. The driver must have done something to the pump. The driver threw the reverser into full forward gear and flung open the regulator. In his haste he had not ensured that the reverser was caught in the notch, so it flew back into full reverse, and with the regulator in full open, the loco accelerated into the waiting

The Gordon Highlander.

coaches. The resulting bang was heard all over Boat of Garten. The coaches received such a thump that they set off towards Aviemore. The startled signalman could see that they were going to be derailed on the catch points so he threw the lever to open the points and the coaches rolled off towards Aviemore, finally coming to a halt on the slight grade. The fireman got out to see what the damage was. The driver's wife, who lived nearby, had heard the bang and had rushed to the station to see what had happened. Together with the driver, she was hastily trying to jam pieces of stick into the holes in the tender. The force of the impact had burst the rivets in the tender and water was pouring out of every hole. The driver shouted to his mate to lend a hand, but the fireman just laughed and declined. He could see that the loco was going nowhere that day, and no amount of sticking twigs into the holes was going to save the water

GNSR locomotive 45 of 'V' Class with old GNSR coaches at the Railway Centenary display at Darlington in 1925. It was scrapped later that year.

"Gordon Highlander' BR 62277 LNER D40 preserved and operational on a special train in 1960s.

supply and the loco would never make Keith. The coach that had received the impact was of the saloon type, and all the seats were jumbled up in one end of the coach. At that time the area was short of coaches, so this was an extra burden.

Of course, a full inquiry was undertaken. The crew and the signalman were given the day off to attend. This was held in the waiting room at the Boat where a large table was set up, with the three officials sitting at it. One by one they were called in to give evidence. Then one by one they were called in again, then a third time. The fireman was closely

Train leaving Boat of Garten 1950s.

examined, and the carefully worded questions were put more bluntly. The driver was reputed to have a liking for a dram; was he drunk at the time of the incident? This was a difficult question, raising all sorts of conflicting loyalties. The fireman replied that he did not know how to define drunk, was it staggering a little? Grasping at blades of grass? Or flat out dead to the world? The inspector lost his temper and accused the fireman of making a mockery of the inquiry and threw him out. In the end the signalman received three days' suspension without pay, the driver two days, and the fireman no penalty. The driver appealed and his punishment was reduced to a day.

With less attention paid to health and safety in those days and more emphasis on personal responsibility to look after yourself, working on the railway could be dangerous. On a winter's day of thick snow and driving wind, the whisky train reached Aviemore and the fireman went to report to the signalbox. He was told that the northbound train was delayed, and they would have to continue towards the Hill and inquire at each signalbox to see where they would cross with the northbound train. Then the crew would change over with the Perth men, each crew returning home on the other's locomotive.

They continued into the dark wild night. After Newtonmore the line is bleak and exposed, and it would not be a good idea to keep stopping at each box, especially at Dalnaspidal, as they could become snow bound.

At Newtonmore the fireman went up into the signalbox to see what the news was. The signalman was busy with a train and would ring Control. While the fireman sat in the nice warm box, quite content to wait there, the door burst open and a distraught Perth driver crashed in. He was in a terrible state, had wet himself, and declared that he had killed a man. The fireman questioned him. He had a van with a 'hot box' in his train. This is where the plain wheel bearings had not been properly greased, or insufficiently greased, and metal was rubbing on metal until it was very hot, and would soon seize and cause great damage. He had been detaching it and shunting it into a siding and had run down two gangers who he had not seen in the dark and the blinding snow, and obviously for the same reason they had not heard or noticed the shunting movement. The fireman rushed over to the yard, shouting to the guard to come and help, which he refused to do, he was staying in his nice warm van. The fireman dragged one of the gangers clear, he was suffering from cuts and bruises but could, shakily, walk, and made his way towards the station. The other man lay between the rails with his arm severed at the shoulder. The fireman dragged him out and lay him in the snow. There was amazingly little blood. It seemed that the wheel flange had neatly severed the arm and crimped the blood vessels, and the cold helped as well. The man was also quite fortified with drink and again this would have helped, although it probably contributed to his not being alert to the shunting movement. The fireman ran to the station building and told the stationmaster to call a doctor and an ambulance. The stationmaster rang, and related that the doctor said that he would not call an ambulance until he had seen the patient himself. The fireman forcibly explained that by the time the doctor had done that the man would be dead, and believe him, the arm was completely off and no doubt about it. The ambulance was called. On a shelf in the office was the stack of blankets and pillows for the blue camping coach that was rented out to holidaymakers in the summer. Camping coaches were an institution and were quite popular at one time, and provided a good use for old coaches that were specially converted and left in sidings at popular stations around the network. The fireman grabbed two blankets to cover the injured man. The stationmaster ordered him to leave them where they were. They were railway property only to be used for the camping coach and were all signed for. A furious argument ensued, and the stationmaster reported the theft of two blankets to the police as the fireman barged out of the door and returned to the injured ganger. By now the man was shaking and he was wrapped carefully in the blankets, still lying in the snow. The ambulance and the doctor arrived. The ambulance could not get down the goods yard because of the snow, so the man was stretchered away.

The Perth crew, shaken, were relieved of their duty and would return home on the first train south. The Speyside men took over the other train and arrived back at Aviemore and went home.

Some days later the Inspector called the fireman into the office and told him that his prompt action had most probably saved the ganger's life, and he was recovering in hospital. He could expect a letter of commendation. The fireman retorted that he would happily forego the letter of commendation if the Inspector would arrange that the charge of theft of two blankets against him would be dropped – which it was.

When the line over the Hill, that is through the Pass of Drumochter is blocked the only alternative is to go through Keith to Aberdeen, and then south via Dundee. In the 1960s diesels arrived, and were hoped to reduce running costs and help keep the lines open. The passenger service on Speyside was put in the hands of light two axle rail buses. Extra halts were opened, and the railbuses had steps that could be lowered at these new halts to let passengers climb on and off. One night, the Hill was shut, and a driver was called out to take a railbus on a special run from Aviemore down to Keith with passengers who were waiting for the sleeper to London. They would connect at Keith with the sleeper, and then continue south. As the driver was going the foreman called him back and gave him a large adjustable wrench, a crow bar, and a big screwdriver. He explained that the gearbox on the railbus was playing up again, and the driver would need these tools to be able to get back. The journey to Keith was uneventful, but there were some soldiers waiting to go back to Aviemore. They piled into the railbus but the driver had to ask a few of them to get out. He unbolted the seat from the floor and removed it. Then he unbolted a panel in the floor and removed it. Then he unbolted the cover on the top of the gearbox and laid it to one side. Then he inserted the crow bar and moved it over into reverse. Now he put it all

The Dufftown to Craigellachie permanent way gang.

M 'Gosh' Hutchen Craig / Dufftown section.

back together again, including the seat. As you can imagine, all this was accompanied by many wise remarks from the soldiers. Having now got it going in the right direction, the driver set off again for Aviemore. He managed to keep it going despite the deepening snow, and finally made Aviemore by crawling along in first gear. On arrival, the railbus was abandoned until the morning, shunting it back into a siding was too much bother.

The railbuses were very light, with only a 125h.p. engine. One ran into a minor landslide caused by the snow and just bounced off the rails, another time it stuck in only moderate snow at Cromdale. They were, however, easy to drive. One driver had gangrene in a finger and drove up and down with the finger in a glass of water on the control panel, to calm down the throbbing pain – something that could never be done on a steam engine.

Scotland was one of the first regions to go over to diesels. The training was simple, the men went to Edinburgh for two weeks of intensive learning, and that was it. It was a lot to take in all at one go, and the diesels were complicated machines compared to steam locomotives. One crew had a Class 24 medium-powered diesel locomotive on the goods, and noticed that the dials were showing that they had a problem, a coolant leak.

They were at Carron, shunting, and reported the problem to the signalbox. Control asked how bad it was. The loco was low on water, and would not be able to continue with the train, but might make it a little way. The plan was to attach it to the front of the passenger train, take it to Imperial, and dump it in the sidings there. This was duly done, and as the crew travelled towards Imperial, the driver was unhappy. He was the secretary of the local railwaymen's Association Mutual Improvement class, and had organised a dance for that night. It was important for him to be there at Aviemore, after all the hard work that he had put into organising the event. With the problem with the 24, they would have to wait for fitters to arrive, goodness knows when they would get home. At the distillery siding, they decided to see what the problem was. After searching through the loco, they traced it to a large four-inch diameter pipe that was cracked at a joint. They went to the distillery to seek help. The still men were happy to assist. They provided some broad thick water proof black sticky tape, and this was liberally wrapped round the pipe and the joint. Then a tarred rope was 'borrowed' off the tarpaulin of a wagon and tightly bound around the joint. They considered this the best that could be done, now to fill it up with water again. The stillmen helped with a hose, there was always plenty of water at a still. The fireman held the big hose into the filling hole, and the stillmen turned it on. The pressure was very high, and it took the unfortunate firemen all his strength to hold it in, and the escaping fountain of water shot up his sleeves and all over him, soaking him through. When it was full, and they went to the signalbox, obtained the token, and set off for Aviemore. At Ballindalloch they stopped to top it up. The signalman told them that they only had six

The Prince Regent at Stirling where it worked the Kinross and Lady bank service from 1934 to 1946.

minutes or they would have to wait until the passenger passed them. The only water available was from an ordinary tap on the platform and a small bore hose, but five minutes of this put a little more water in, and off they dashed again. They reached Aviemore, and parked the diesel, reporting the fault and going off to get cleaned up for the dance. They were most surprised to subsequently receive a letter of commendation. Apparently, they were the first crew to repair a diesel loco out on the line and get it

M79972 when new. At one time it worked the Speyside line.

Railbus M79972 at Grantown East.

home again, rather than just declare it a cripple and sit and wait for help. Little did authority know that it was the dance that provided the spur to their dedication.

The speed of the goods train, and so the service quality offered to the distillery customers was not enhanced when the diesel locomotives arrived. To keep costs down, the Class 08 shunting diesel locomotives, with 0-6-0 wheel arrangement and a top speed of around 20m.p.h. were

D 6128 at Keith 0n 4/5/68.

The 0840 SO Keith Town/Aberdeen leaves Keith Junctiom for Keith Town on the last day 4/5/68.

put on the job. The run was from Elgin to Craigellachie, then to Boat of Garten, back to Craigellachie and then via Dufftown to Keith. This took all day, even if there was not a lot of shunting to be done at all the various distillery sidings. The engines had to go to Inverness at the weekends for servicing and again, this would take forever. One loco was going from Aviemore on the direct route to Inverness for its service and the driver was just frustrated with the slow progress and opened it up to flat-out. The engine didn't like this, it was not designed for sustained flat-out running and it seized solid at Slochd. There was nothing that could be done with it, so a relief engine was sent from Inverness with some drums of oil. The rails were covered with oil and the 08 dragged along until it could be slid into the relief siding at the summit. Fitters were sent to free it and it was then towed to Inverness for repair. Common sense prevailed and the shunters were replaced on the goods duties with more suitable locomotives, but their time on the service did nothing to help retain freight on the railway, especially as road haulage was becoming increasingly effective competition.

D6128 and D5342 @ Keith on 4/5/68.

The period of change from steam to diesel was not a happy one. The limited training was not enough to absorb all the complexities of the new method of traction but with the resourcefulness inbred in the railwaymen they adapted and took to the new locos. They were certainly cleaner and easier than steam locos, and the cabs were more comfortable. One driver recalled when he was on a Black Five which was being piloted by a 'Barney' 0-6-0 over Dava Moor because of the snow on the exposed section of the line across the moor. (Loco crews tended to call all 0-6-0 tender engines 'Barneys' even though it was a Highland Railway term) As they ploughed through the drifts he saw the snow sliding along the roof of the loco. Unfortunately, the roof hatch was open by about four inches. The snow was forced down into the cab and all over the crew. It then melted and by the time the men arrived at Forres they were soaked – there was no protective clothing issued in those days. The diesels are more temperamental than steam locos, and when something went wrong, even a little thing, it would disable the engine. Steam locos could usually be persuaded to limp home. One steam tender engine suffered a collapse on part of the valve gear on one side, which brought it to a halt. Although it was possible to limp home on one cylinder, it was dangerous with the damaged gear. The fireman attacked it with a hammer and freed off the damaged rod. After careful consideration the crew worked out that if the fireman held a metal bar in the gear this would get it working. He would have to simply remove the bar quickly once it was moving and climb onto the engine as it moved off. This they did and made it to the next station. Passengers were leaning out of the windows to see why the train was lurching along with such a forward-and-aft motion. Once again the fireman performed the dangerous operation with the bar and off they went. Keith Depot was alerted by the signalman to send a relief loco to Craigellachie to take over the train. Three times the fireman dangerously restarted the train and they limped into Craigellachie. To the crews frustration there was no sign of a relief loco. It transpired that Keith had not believed the story. If a loco was that badly damaged, it would have failed and that would be the end of it. However, as the train was clearly working it must be fit to make it all the way to Keith Depot and the signalman must have been exaggerating. The train was abandoned at 'The Craig'.

The B12 4-6-0s were very popular engines on the line. They were nicknamed 'hikers' as with their power they could pull anything, anywhere. There are a few versions of how they gained their nickname. One is that some of them were fitted for a while with feed water heaters. These were cylinders strapped to the top of the boiler behind the chimney. With all the associated plumbing hanging down, it looked like they were wearing rucksacks. Another version is that the distance from the tender to the firebox was much more than normally found on GNSR locos, and so the firemen had to walk back and forward each time they threw a shovel full of coal on the fire, making them hike. Yet another version is that with their big wheels and free flowing action, they could go anywhere with the ease of a hiker. They were designed by S. D. Holden for the Great Eastern Railway, and were sent north to help with a shortage of powerful engines. The very last one was working up to Aviemore when the big end on one cylinder broke, bringing the train to a rapid halt in the mid-section before Cromdale. Quick as a flash, the fireman grabbed the single line token, jumped down off the loco and ran up the banking, cleared the fence and flagged down a passing bus. The crew had seen the bus earlier and just at that point the road and railway were parallel. The signalman at Boat of Garten couldn't believe it when the fireman walked in with the token, but without the train. He thought that it was some sort of leg-pull when the fireman explained that he had caught the bus. The plan was to send down a rescue loco with drums of oil to go on the rails. Then the B12 would be dragged, with its motion locked up, to the nearest siding and dumped. Due to a gap in communications the loco depot could not understand why four drums of oil were needed, so none was sent. The B12 was dragged, squealing, on dry rails, to the siding and left for recovery later.

Towards the end of steam, repairs were not authorised on the locos and standards of maintenance fell. This is not surprising, as depots were closing and jobs disappearing in the hundreds. The railway provided employment for so many people in the rural areas of Speyside. At one time in Keith more than 300 men and women were employed in the two loco sheds, the stations and the goods yards, which were busy 24 hours a day. It was unsocial work too; shifts were long and hard, the work usually dirty but it created a great 'belonging' in the railway men and women. The conditions would just not be accepted today. The drivers' bothy at Boat of Garten was a brick room with a fire and a bench. There were no canteen facilities, sandwiches were eaten when they could, usually out on the line. The Bothy was, one day, most unexpectedly painted cream. It was believed that it had never been painted since it was built. The fire-raiser decided to build up the fire in this nice, shiny, clean bothy and have a snooze. The coal just then was imported Polish nuts. These burned very hot but fused together to form huge chunks of clinker that required a lot of poking with a big bar by the fireman to break up and keep the locos' firebox working properly. The fire-raiser built up a great haystack of Polish nuts and settled down in the snug, warm, bothy in front of the big glowing fire. Unfortunately, for him the foreman came looking for him, found him fast asleep and roared at him to get up and work. The fire-raiser, frightened out of a deep sleep, jumped up half awake and threw the contents of his bucket on the fire and rushed out. In the bucket were his materials of paraffin soaked rags, and sticks. The fire exploded into flame which reached across the ceiling and out the door. The bothy was black. Later, the inspector arrived and looked into the blackened bothy. "Anybody hurt?" he asked. On being assured that no one had been hurt, he walked away. The men could sort it out themselves. The bothy was still black when it was demolished.

The B12 61504 leaves Keith Junction on an up passenger from the Glen line.

There were plenty of characters working on the line, including a permanent way supervisor with a sense of humour. When there was work on the line, a temporary speed restriction would be imposed until the track was judged to be fit for normal working. The temporary speed limit signs were numbers cut out of hardboard and placed on a pole by the track and painted yellow. These were not very robust and could break with the force of the wind and weather. At one time there were two speed

The D6149 Class 21 at Huntly on an up passenger 1963.

restrictions in force on the supervisor's stretch of the line, one to 25m.p.h. and one to 35m.p.h. In both cases the number 5 had snapped and the supervisor asked Craigellachie to send him up two more number 5s. A packet arrived, but it only contained one number 5. The supervisor was not a particularly lettered man and painstakingly printed out a message to be sent down to Craigellachie. He asked: "What's this one five four – is it for the 25 at Advie or the 35 at Cromdale?" Craigellachie duly sent another 5 up to him with a response that he could please himself which 5 he used where.

The permanent way men were out in all weathers maintaining the track. In the winter they would get a warm up and have their 'piece' in the permanent way huts, which were situated beside the track, heated by a small stove. The coal for the fire was thrown to them from a passing locomotive. One day (the train engine was a K2 with the driver on the 'wrong' side) a driver saw a ganger by his hut waving his arms from over his head down to the ground indicating that he would like some coal for his stove. The fireman usually obliged, but with the driver being on that side, he quickly turned and grabbed a big slab of coal, about the size of the top of a coffee table and threw it out of the cab. Then he cried out in horror imagining that he was going to kill the ganger as he could see the big slab of coal flying through the air straight towards the ganger who had little room to jump out of the way, especially with the train bearing down on him. The fireman rushed across the cab and the crew watched as, arms outstretched like a goal keeper, legs apart, the ganger jumped to the left, then the right, as he tried to quickly work out the trajectory of the slab of coal. Finally, he jumped clean into the air and the slab passed between his legs and smashed onto the ground. At least the exercise would have warmed him up and he would have a good supply of coal.

Boat of Garten was a junction with the direct line to Forres over Dava Moor, the original Highland Railway route to Inverness, running alongside the GNSR line to Craigellachie for a while before they diverge. Trains going to Aviemore by both routes were timed to make connections with each other and sometimes they resulted in a race to reach Boat of Garten first. From Broomhill Station the crew could see Nethybridge Station and would look out for the tell-tale plume of steam that would indicate that the two trains were running almost together for a time and a race would take place. The GNSR 4-4-0s were affectionately known as 'Tin-Charlies' as they resembled the tin plate, spindly Hornby 'O' gauge toy locomotives, more than the solid more modern locos. The GNSR D41s could often show even the splendid Black 5 4-6-0s a clean pair of heels in the race to Boat of Garten. One driver had set his mind on having a race, but on reaching Broomhill they could see no sign of the other train. He decided to have a race anyway. They set off in grand style and then the driver pushed the regulator all the way open and the loco roared away – much to the despair of the fireman. The engine was due to finish its turn of duty at Boat of Garten and go in the shed, so the fireman had

been running down the fire, leaving just a thin covering to keep enough
steam to reach the Boat. The driver's enthusiastic driving lifted the fire
and blew it straight out of the chimney in showers of red-hot sparks and
cinders. This caused the boiler pressure to fall away until the loco slowed
and came to a halt just short of the Boat of Garten platform, with the crew
hastily trying to build enough fire to raise a bit more steam. The guard
came up to see what was wrong, while passengers climbed down onto the
track and walked along to the station. When enough steam was raised the
red faced crew shuffled the train into the station.

  Some of the events on the line were humorous, but could be dangerous.
Early one morning at Boat of Garten, the crew booked on at 3a.m. and
prepared a Black 5. The first job was to steam heat the five coaches for
the train down Speyside that set off after the 1.10a.m. from Perth to
Inverness, and made a connection with it, at Aviemore. They set off with
the empty train to Aviemore to await the connection. It was still dark
when they left Aviemore at 4.40a.m. and ran down to Boat of Garten. The
driver was renowned for being hard on the engine and the fireman, so the
fire was kept well up to try to keep it all in the grate and not out of the
chimney, and to supply the steam that the driver always managed to use.
There was a lengthy stop at the Boat while mailbags and bundles of
newspapers were put out onto the platform, the guard gave a green light
and the driver rammed open the regulator. To his surprise, nothing
happened. The crew checked their gauges, and found that instead of the
necessary 21 inches of vacuum, the dial only showed 15inches, so the
brakes would not come off. They decided that they had better check the
engine. The fireman lit the oil lamp and climbed down between the
engine and the first coach, shouting to the guard that they had no vacuum
and he was going to check the coupling. He uncoupled the vacuum pipe
from the coach and sealed it on the engine coupling. The driver
confirmed that the engine was okay, and took the lamp and said that he
was going back to check the coaches. The fireman recoupled the pipe to
the coach, put the pin in place to secure the ends, and just as he climbed
back up onto the platform he heard the piston working in the vacuum
pump and the train started to move off. The driver was still down the
platform somewhere. The fireman set off running down the platform end
slope, luckily he could just see the tender handrail in the glow from the
firebox and made a jump for it, swung himself aboard and stopped the
train. The driver came running up white as a sheet. When the train had set
off, he was too far along it to have a chance of reaching the engine, so he
had quickly opened a door and jumped into a coach with the intention of
stopping the train with the emergency cord. When the fireman had
shouted to the guard, he had gone to check the rear coach and found that
the vacuum pipe was not secured to the dummy plug. He had secured it
and put the pin in place. The engine had then made the vacuum, the
brakes had released, and because the driver had wrongly left the regulator
wide open, the train set off.

WORKING ON THE RAILWAY

RAILWAYS can be dangerous places to work. A relief porter was needed at Boat of Garten This was a joint station shared with the LMS, and each railway had its own staff there. The relief porter was needed to replace a LNER man, and so the relief man had to be provided from an LNER station. The chosen man was from Elgin and had to go up on the first train in the morning. This was a train that originated from Inverness, and ran through to Elgin where the porter joined it for the run up Speyside. It was dark, but fine as the train made its way towards Elgin. At the western end of Elgin there is a level crossing with a signal box. The box has the usual little platform for the signalman to stand on with his arms out to receive the hooped pouch with the token in it for the section from Forres and with his other hand giving out the hooped pouch with the token for the next station, which the fireman scooped up in his arms. The train was booked to pass the level crossing at 5.55a.m. and it was a regular feature to see the night-watchman from the adjacent sawmill standing with his bicycle waiting to cross the line to go home, the crew never had the time to acknowledge him. The fireman was watching carefully to ensure that the token pouch hoops were aligned with those of the signalman to ensure an effective change-over, otherwise the train had to stop and he would have to run back to the box to make the change-over. The driver was carefully regulating the speed, too fast and the fireman or the signalman could have a broken arm. They rolled in to the Elgin GNSR station and gently came to a halt. The relief porter was waiting there and asked the crew: "You've surely nae much faith in your loco today, then?" They were puzzled and asked what he was getting at. "The bike on the front." They went to look and sure enough, a bicycle was jammed at the front of the engine and a cloth cap. It was the cap of the night-watchman, they had run him down without knowing.

The same driver had another unfortunate experience not long afterwards. He was acting foreman at the engine shed at the Boat of Garten on the back shift (2p.m. to 10p.m.). It was a time of snow and his night shift counterpart came on early to let him get away home as he had to cycle to Aviemore. On this day, his relief was overdue and he wondered why he was late. The railbus came into the shed at the end of a run and the driver came into the shed and called his mate to come and see, it looked like someone was lying in the snow. It was the night shift foreman who had taken a heart attack and was lying dead, face down in the snow. This was quite upsetting to the railbus driver, so the acting foreman took charge. He sent the driver to get a stretcher, then he rang the signalbox to tell them what had happened and that he would bring the body over in the rail bus to the station. It would be easier than walking through the snow and would protect the body from the elements. The signalman set the points, they opened the railbus door and went for the stretcher with the body on it. As they were lifting it to the door, one of the dead man's arms slipped off the stretcher and swung down, this caused an escape of air from the lungs and a noise from the throat. This greatly frightened the driver who let go of his end, leaving it propped on the door frame. The acting foreman was suddenly left holding up his end of the stretcher at shoulder height with the body slipping towards him. He roared at the driver, who pulled himself together, and they slipped the stretcher into the railbus. The foreman carefully drove the railbus to the station and the body was removed to the waiting room until the doctor arrived, and the ambulance. He then went to the cab at the other end and set off back across to the depot. Suddenly, he saw the driver's heavy serge coat lying between the rails – he had run him over. In a panic he stopped the railbus and got out to find the other driver's body, it was not there – he was already back at the shed. It transpired that he had draped his big coat over the front of the radiator of the railbus to protect it from the cold as he drove up the line in it and the coat had slipped off as the railbus was going over to the station. What a relief – he thought that as things came in three's this was the third body he would have to deal with, fortunately it was not to be.

His theory that things came in three's was borne out by another incident. At Invergordon there used to be an aluminium smelter and they received cement in hopper wagons. One day when the wagons were being shunted the driver made a mistake, he thought that he was reversing into a loop when the points were critically set for a dead-end siding. The wagons were pushed with some force through the buffer stops and ended up with the last one partly in the air. The carriage and wagon examiner was surprised to find that there was hardly any damage to be seen on the wagons, although the buffer stops were completely wrecked. The wagons were carefully drawn away and another examination revealed the only damage was one buffer face that was bent at the top, which could quite easily be repaired. These were private owner wagons belonging to Portland Cement and were duly returned to Oxwellmains, near Dunbar, the loading point south of Edinburgh. A report was made and a copy sent to the cement company. No more was heard and it was assumed that the repair had been made and not recharged to the railway, or even just left as it was. Then, after six months, a claim arrived. This was followed up by the railway, why so long in claiming? It was reported that the original paperwork had been received at the cement works, signed for and put in a desk drawer by the supervisor. He had then gone home and died in his sleep that night. For six months the job had been covered by other people until a replacement was appointed. He went through the desk, found the papers, and submitted the claim.

Our man at Boat of Garten was convinced he was a jinx. While he was there 'Glen Douglas' (a favourite GNSR 4-4-0 engine) was backed into the shed too fast and demolished the rear wall. As usual there was an inquiry and a letter of reprimand. The railway masons were sent for to rebuild the wall. Within 24 hours, with the cement not even dry, another careless driver had again backed 'Glen Douglas' through the bricks. It is

North British Glen Class LNER D34 'Glen Falloch' on Hawick shed.

believed that the hole stayed there until the shed was closed.

In the early 1960s BR was getting rid of thousands of old wagons and coaches. The bodies were sold far and wide and it is rare to find a farm in the North East that does not have at least one van body, somewhere, although the ravages of time, weather and neglect are rapidly reducing the amount of them. The carriage and wagon store at Boat of Garten was an old coach body, a full-length coach, resting on the two longitudinal oak beams. This was sold to a farmer who wanted to use it as a hen house. It is believed that he still has it. The farmer asked the railwaymen if they could arrange to deliver it for him, for a suitable recompense. Much thought went into this. It is not easy to find cranes and low loader lorries and they are expensive. A plan was hatched. The roads were covered in hard-packed snow and ice – gritting was not done then. They would drag the coach like a big sledge. The local constable was consulted about the legality of such a move and he was certain that it could not be done. It would damage the road and break several laws, for sure, although he did not know what they were, he was sure that there were laws about such things and it just could not be done. The railwaymen tried to think of alternatives but could not.

Then there was a stroke of luck, the policeman was going away to the West Coast for a few days' holiday. The railwaymen decided that they would deliver the coach that night. A Fordson Major tractor was borrowed and chains attached to the coach. Just to be sure the railway red tail lamp was attached to the rear of the coach and off they set. The coach glided along well on its runners, the exit from the yard is down a slope which posed no problem. At the bottom they joined the road and had to make a sharp left turn to go under the railway bridge. The coach body had a bit of momentum on it by now and slid across the road and bounced off the bank. The tractor tugged and it obligingly swung round and was effortlessly pulled under the bridge. Almost immediately there is a T-junction, and again the coach was swung round this with no difficulty. They now set off past the Loch and up to the main road junction by the sawmill. This is on a gradually increasing gradient and just at the T-junction onto the main road they might have to stop if there happened to be any traffic. They wondered if they would need another tractor to help pull it round, but the Fordson plodded on and they successfully negotiated the corner.

On the main road the bizarre convoy set off until they reached the narrow opening to the farm track. They stopped and studied the lie of the land. On the corner stood a stout telegraph pole. They pulled forward, swung round, and pivoted the coach against the telegraph pole, which fortunately, withstood the strain. Then it was off up to the farm. The coach was left in the courtyard for the farmer to drag it to wherever he wanted to put it. The Fordson was returned to its home, and altogether a good night's work was done.

Emboldened by their success, and taking advantage of the hard-packed snow, they repeated the operation another night, this time with a short coach body that another farmer had bought. This was much easier to manoeuvre and the farm was reached by dragging the body over the moor. This was proving to be quite a profitable sideline.

Then the policeman came back. Now it is just not possible to have a big Fordson Major tractor roaring through the village in the middle of the night dragging a coach body without everyone knowing about it. However, finding someone to give evidence might be more difficult. The policeman went to see the railwaymen and told them that he knew what they had been up to, and he would make sure that they were prosecuted somehow. He was in a fine rage and felt that he was being made to look a fool. The railwaymen protested their innocence, they had done nothing wrong. The policeman had said that they couldn't do it, and they had merely proved that they *could* do it, that was all. The policeman had never said that they *must* not do it. The policeman was furious at this deliberate and cheeky misinterpretation of what he had said, and repeated that he was away to start an investigation and he would get them. The railwaymen casually asked him how his back was. The policeman froze – why were they asking after his back? The railwaymen replied that they had heard rumours about some frolics that some policemen had been up to on the West Coast, some frolics that higher authority in the police would most certainly be upset to hear about. Almost bursting with frustration the policeman turned and marched away. No more was heard of prosecutions.

Probably the most vital piece of equipment to a railwayman is the tail lamp. If a train is seen without a tail lamp the signalman must assume that some part of it has broken loose and is fouling the line and urgent action is taken. All trains must have a tail lamp – the only exception is the Royal train, which must have two tail lamps. The Royal train also has it's own telegraph code. In these days of instant communication, it is difficult to appreciate the importance that the telegraph had. One young lady left school at $14^1/_2$, which was not at all unusual, because her father, who worked on the railway as a signalman, had heard of the vacancy for a clerk and managed to get her the job. She had to learn the telegraph and was sent to Aberdeen for instruction. She was fortunate in having a father who knew the telegraph code as he had to use it to communicate with the signal boxes on either side of him. At home in the evenings he used to tap

The 65288, North British 0-6-0 LNER J36 at Hawick.

the poker on the fire side in the letters of the alphabet and kept testing his daughter until she became proficient.

Telegraph users all had their little idiosyncrasies and experienced operators could tell who was on the line. The girl worked in the office at Kintore where her father was on the signal box. In slack moments he would telegraph a message to her to encourage her. Clerks were never issued with uniforms. One of her jobs was to go down the yard every morning and note down the number of each wagon there and then telegraph this information to Aberdeen. When she had a transfer to Aberdeen she was paid 30/- (£1.50) a week and found that after she had paid for her digs, the attraction of the big shops soon took up all her money. However, come what may, she always kept 1/6 ($7^1/_2$p) in reserve to buy stockings. Clambering around in the goods yards, particularly in the dark mornings, usually resulted in a laddered stocking that had to be replaced quickly. In Aberdeen telegraph office around 50 operators manned the banks of machines, sending and receiving messages, instructions, returns and statistics constantly.

After a while, her father moved to Rothes. He was still a signalman but the job at Rothes paid 1/- (5p) a week more and that was enough to warrant the move. The box was manned on two shifts and was kept immaculate. The floor was spotless and polished, the men used rags to burnish the lever handles, everything glowed and shone. No-one was allowed to touch the levers with their bare hands as it would tarnish them. Most signal boxes were kept as spotless as this, even though people would come in and out and there was a coal fire in it. Her mother complained that her father never did any work around the house and was untidy, but his box was perfect! The girl was a relief clerk for a year and this entailed her working wherever needed, including Aberdeen (where she found lodgings in Union Street), Port Elphinstone, which was always busy with paper traffic, Elgin, Lossiemouth, Inverurie, Keith Town and Keith Junction. She was usually a little pressed for time in the mornings

The Tomintoul bus with driver William Low at Dufftown Station.

and would arrive at the station with the hair rollers still in, tied up with a turban. A quick sign-on, splash of water on the face and dismantling of the headgear sufficed to be ready for the day's work.

She also worked at Dufftown Station which had its own rush hour. Every morning Low's bus would arrive from Tomintoul packed with people coming to take the train. It was accompanied by Michies bus from the Commercial Hotel bringing the town's folk to the station and it too was packed. The buses also brought parcels. A porter would have to weigh each one on the platform scale and then the clerk could calculate the charge. Small packets were weighed inside the booking office. There were always parcels of all sorts, including spare parts for distillery machinery, household goods or clothes sent out from Aberdeen; boxes of day-old chicks – just about everything. This was a little after 7a.m. and both buses were there again in the evening to take the crowds home again from their work. It was at Dufftown that she first came across the 'dog'.

This was a clever device like a small diameter pipe sharpened at one end. This would be hammered into a cask and a straw pushed through into the whisky. When the thief had drunk all he wanted, he carefully withdrew the 'dog' and the whisky impregnated oak stave would seal itself up again. Eventually, she was to be married – to a young railwayman, of course – whose father was also a signalman at Rothes on the opposite shift to her father. This meant that on the day of the wedding two relief signalmen were needed at Rothes. When the happy couple set off on the train for their honeymoon in Glasgow, the train ran from Rothes to Craigellachie to a cacophony of explosions as the railwaymen had placed detonators at intervals all along the line – this was not reported to authority.

The intensity of railway operations before the war is difficult to imagine now. Just about everything went by train, life was adapted to this, just as today it is adapted to the car and the lorry. Apart from the whisky casks and draff, all the sundry items also came and went by train. A good example is to look at one week in August 1933. In addition to the normal train service, the following specials were organised in the week ending August 11. It shows the manpower and machinery that was available and mobilised, all as a matter of course.

Despite it being a peak season, normal track repairs and renewals carried on as usual, and the gangers were working between Rothes and Coleburn, Kemnay and Monymusk, Pitfodels and Cults, and Park and Drum. Each of these involved speed restrictions for passing trains. It was noted on the notices that a "portable telephone would be placed in the signal boxes at Rothes, Holburn Street and Culter in connection with these works". To get the workers to and from these sites, an extra coach was attached to goods trains, with stops made specially to set down, and later pick-up, the men. It was noted that a goods train from Maud to Kittybrewster would have to be shunted out of the way 'as required' to let the fish train from Fraserburgh/Peterhead to pass it. Fish traffic received top priority. Several parties were catered for including 48 Scots Guards travelling from Aberdeen to Ballater; a Mr. Mellis with four adults and 40 children going from Holburn Street, Aberdeen to Murtle; 1000 adults and 500 children in a 'Fish Trades' outing from Aberdeen to Milltimber and 75 adults and 150 children from the Caledonian Order of Oddfellows going from Aberdeen to Dyce. All these parties were travelling out and back on Saturday, August 5, and instructions were given that 10 adults and 16 juveniles were to be fitted into each compartment and stationmasters had to ensure that the person in charge of each party was told the time when the return train would leave. Presumably, in preparation for the 'Glorious 12th', a Lieut. Col. Wheatley's establishment was travelling from Berkswell to Knockando. This party travelled in a bogie brake van, a composite sleeper (presumably First Class for the party and Second Class for the servants) with an 'aeroplane van'. This van, containing two motor cars, was to be placed on the loading bank at Craigellachie and the cars unloaded promptly. The brake van (presuma-

D30 No. 62440 'Wandering Wullie' at Hawick.

bly, with all the luggage) and the sleeping car continued to the private Knockando House Halt where a special stop would be made for detraining. The van and sleeper continued to Boat of Garten for handing back to the LMS.

Insch Show was on and special trains were run from Inverurie and Pitcaple with horse boxes, which ran back again in the evening. Special trains for day trips also arrived in Aberdeen from Perth (Messrs. Pullars excursion, a staff outing?) Hawick, Galashiels, Edinburgh, Alloa and Alva. All this involved an enormous amount of organisation.

Over the rest of the week a similar high level of activity included Aboyne Blue Triangle Club, 40 people day trip Aberdeen to Inverness, and 120 Freemasons from Kintore to Inverness. The theatrical company 'Back to Nature' of 30 people with a 45ft.-long 'covcar' van with props departed for London, Kings Cross. Chief Constable Stewart organised a party of 20 adults and 260 children for a day trip from Elgin to Lossiemouth. An open excursion was run from Forres for a day in Aberdeen, picking up also at Keith. Aberlour and Dufftown had a Monday holiday, so a special excursion was run to Aberdeen and back. Another was run from and to Fraserburgh to cater for Lonmay and Auchnagatt local holidays. The Great Keith Show was on the Tuesday, as were agricultural shows in Turriff and Alford. All these required special trains to move the livestock. The Keith Show is always important and the volume of traffic meant that all other goods traffic would be placed in sidings at Cairnie to free up space at Keith. Special trains also ran from Knockando to Keith and along the coast line.

On the Wednesday, similar arrangements were made for sales at

The 80114 climbs out of Craigellachie.

Banchory, Maud and Huntly. Another group 'Bessemers' Party' travelled from London King's Cross to Ballater, with their composite sleeper being transferred off the London train onto the Deeside train. It was also Banff Flower Show and Highland Games, necessitating another special train, while another open excursion ran from Aberdeen to Elgin and back, via Keith and Dufftown on the way out, returning via the coast. This must have been a heavy train as it is specifically noted that a B12 4-6-0 must be rostered for this train and was expected to run in two portions because of the demand. This train left Aberdeen at 4.55a.m. with the return arriving back at 10.31p.m.. A long day out! A special was also run from Macduff to and from Aberdeen, and Aberdeen to Dundee and back.

Thursday dawned with sales at Cornhill, Inverurie and Turriff with another shoal of specials together with a Methodist Mission Party day trip from Aberdeen to Inverness who required a dining car for outward and return journeys. Other open excursions were run to Macduff and back and Ballater and back. On Friday, arrangements were also made for the 7.50a.m. to stop specially at Kennethmont to set down five Third Class passengers of Reginald Abel Smith's party who had travelled from London on the sleeping car, which went through to Lossiemouth. Another special arrangement was for Kershaw's Establishment who were travelling from Macclesfield to Mintlaw in a composite sleeper and two vans. Another traffic that has long been given up by the railways is pigeons, sent to far away places and released for the race home. A bogie van was to be added to the 17.15p.m. fish train to be loaded with pigeon baskets at Arbroath for delivery to Longtown, Cumbria. Another excursion was run to Ballater and back. The English Bank Holiday was looming and the companies would be running so many specials that they would not take goods traffic unless previously agreed, so more special arrangements had to be made.

The railway clearly catered very well for its market and this shows how adaptable the system was. This excellent provision of transport encouraged and facilitated the growth of distilleries.

The demands of the railway meant that people usually seemed to be travelling to and from their place of work, which frequently varied. For example, a Keith man was given a position at Ballindalloch. For the early turn he would leave Keith around 10p.m. the night before and cycle the long weary miles. The pay structure allowed 'walking money' which was either at pence per mile or hours, for example, a 15-mile journey might be calculated at eight hours' payment. This was one way, the same would be allowed at the end of the week to get back home, and overnight money paid for each night between the weekends. Railwaymen could get home and travel to and fro, depending on the location of the duty and the availability of transport, but the overnight money would still be paid. The only way to avoid the travelling was to find digs near the signing-on point and this was always a problem. Two young clerkesses, finding digs in Keith that they could afford to be scarce, had to end up sleeping in the same bed. In those days this was not a problem and did not have the overtones that would be invoked today.

Working on the railway was always a demanding job and the duty always took precedence over personal likes or dislikes. It did engender a great feeling of belonging to a big extended family and most employees who today are retired, look back with affection at the fun that they had, despite the long and unsocial hours and the low pay.

The railway employed a huge number of people, ranging from the well known loco-crews and station staff through to the permanent way gangs and plumbers, electricians, carpenters and masons who kept the fabric of the railway together.

This army of people were moved around a lot. One young girl who started work at age 15 in 1943 at Cromdale as a passenger clerkess, was soon moved to Ballindalloch to learn the telegraph. This meant obtaining lodgings at Ballindalloch. It was not possible to commute as she had to be there before the first train, or, if working the other shift, after the last train had departed. If another railway employee had a spare room it was a useful source of additional income to provide lodgings for a colleague and the young girl was put in touch with someone and arrangements made. Ballindalloch Station had a special telephone connected directly to Ballindalloch Castle so that any goods or parcels arriving could be advised and the chauffeur arrive to collect them, or Sir George MacPherson Grant could ring when he arrived home by train and the chauffeur would come and collect him. The station also handled a steady traffic of baskets of rabbits, hares and pigeons from the Glenlivet area destined for the London market. No doubt, they fetched a good price during the war. There was also the twice-yearly sheep sales and the general whisky related traffic.

Two soldiers were stationed in a Nissen hut in the railway yard, controlling the military stores for the men. One day one of them came up to the station and said that everyone should go to their hut at 11a.m. to listen to a special broadcast. It was Winston Churchill announcing the D-Day invasion. Everyone was so happy, and the young clerkess was given the rest of the day off to go home and celebrate with her family. She was even given a ride on the footplate of the loco of the next train, with her bicycle carried in the guard's van. The crew even stopped the train as close as possible to her home and helped her and her bicycle up the embankment and over the fence.

Another duty meant that she had to cycle from Cromdale to Craigellachie for her shift and then cycle back, quite a distance in all weathers. One morning she set off and had got about halfway when the vanity of not wanting to wear cycle clips proved a folly when her trouser leg became caught on the pedal wheel and the leg was torn to the knee. She returned home and rang in to explain why she would be late. Fortunately, the stationmaster was good humoured and let her off.

Moving around the system as duties required, she was sent to relieve at Elgin for a weekend. On asking there she was advised to see a certain lady who had a room that she let to railway people. Over the weekend, fish was served up seven times for meals! Obviously, the lady had relatives on the trawlers. The fish diet was perfectly acceptable, but the lassie was glad that it was only for a weekend. Then she was sent to Keith and lodgings proved difficult to find due to the large number of railway people working there, more than 300 in total. Lodgings were found with a kind lady who looked after her well, but the house was very old and infested with cockroaches. She spent the off-duty hours sitting with her feet tucked up under her on the chair out of the way of the insects. As soon as another lodging could be found she moved. It was also difficult as women were paid far less than the men who could pay more and so obtained lodgings in preference to women.

The new lodgings were with a lady who had two rooms available. The girl had one while the other was slept in by a guard during the day and a fireman at night, as they had complementary shift duties. It was at Keith that the lassie was working in a booking office at Keith Town Station. She sat at one end, while the goods clerkess sat at the other. In the middle was one male ticket clerk. One day, while cashing-up, the booking clerk announced that the takings were more than £100. None of them had seen £100 before. The clerk bundled the notes up with rubber bands and the three of them played football with it! At Keith Junction the wages were made up for the loco depot men. The lassie had to sit at a specific window and the men would come up and quote their code number, which had to correspond with the number on the wages sheet. Then she gave the man his tin with his wages in it. He emptied the tin and returned it to her.

Employing so many people meant that a wide variety of skills, talents and characters were present. Many railwaymen served as local

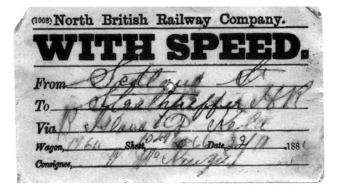

Some historical tickets – many from long gone stations.

councillors, Justices of the Peace or on committees of societies and associations. The low pay meant that their sidelines were often found to augment the family income. A Ballindalloch signalman had a very popular dance band. Others kept hens, or grew vegetables or did part time jobs.

The social side was important and railway social clubs were in every main centre, including Keith, where it still operates, and there were dances up and down the system. For example, there was a big granary at Ballindalloch and during the 'off' season dances were held in it, said to raise money to build Foresterhill Hospital in Aberdeen. Some of the characters were a little worrying, like the guard at Dufftown who took his rifle to work every day to shoot the crows at Glenfiddich Distillery.

The coalmines seemed to have an insatiable appetite for pit props and this provided enough traffic for a special train to run early every morning. During the war there were many sawmills in the area. Unlike today, where the timber is brought to the mill, in those days a forest would be purchased and a mill set up onsite. The workers' houses were timber sections bolted together and these would be erected at a suitable site nearby. The interiors would receive a new coat of paper and paint and be 'home from home' again. Dry toilets would be created in the same field and a nearby burn dammed to create a pool for the water supply. For a period of three years a sawmill was established near Mulben Station, between Keith and Elgin on the Highland route, and the sawmill workers were very pleased to receive hot water once a week from the locomotive to do the washing, it saved a lot of carrying from the burn and heating it up.

The vital connection between distillery and railway varied from road vehicles, which involved manual transhipment at the station, or a siding, or even a small network of lines. On Speyside, Daluaine had exchange sidings, but Balmenach did not, its puggie had to go out into the real railway to reach the sidings. This meant that the loco crew had to be fully conversant with railway rules and systems. In the working timetable the names of the three drivers and two firemen who were passed out to do this were listed, to ensure that no mistakes were made. Once a year an inspector had to travel from Aberdeen to test the men in their knowledge and sign their ticket for another year. A passenger train, coming from Boat of Garten, was told to pick up the inspector at Cromdale station. The crew found him propped on a bench, drunk with a bottle of whisky jutting out of each side pocket in his railway overcoat. The porter helped the driver and fireman load the man onto the footplate where he was unceremoniously dumped in a corner out of the way. There he stayed until Aberlour when he regained consciousness and started to roar. Fortunately, he could not get up as his trousers were caught on a handle on the tender. The crew did not want him causing havoc so they just ignored him. He roared and cursed for a while then fell asleep again. At Craigellachie they had to transfer him to the Aberdeen train that was coming from Elgin. They did not fancy manhandling the big lump from

Signalman Charlie Grant and fotplateman Stanley Watt at Dufftown.

Two unknowns with driver D, Jamieson (right)

one platform to the other, and were concerned in case they broke one of the bottles of whisky as they would surely get the blame and be persecuted by the inspector. They uncoupled their loco and drew forward. When the Aberdeen train came in, they eased up alongside with the help of the Keith crew in the other loco, transferred the inspector across to the other footplate and were glad to see the back of him. They were sure that the liberal hospitality at the distillery had ensured that the signature had been obtained to pass the crew for another year without any actual examination.

The resourcefulness of the railwaymen and the simple dedication of just getting on with the job is well illustrated by the time when the Speyside train came round a curve and found a man standing in the middle of the track, wildly and frantically waving his jacket over his head. The crew slammed on the brakes and swiftly brought the train to a halt. The man ran up and explained that his lorry was stuck on the level crossing ahead. Cautiously, they eased the train forward and up to the crossing. The lorry was moving a farmer to his new farm and was overloaded. The level crossing was higher than the road at each side and so the lorry had bottomed itself on the track. The train crew were not impressed. The driver asked the lorry driver for his jack. For some reason the lorry driver was reluctant to get out the jack but was soon persuaded. The driver and fireman jacked up the rear of the lorry, packed bits of wood under the wheels and the lorry driver carefully drove off. The driver and fireman cleared the wood out of the way and returned to their train and carried on. What the reluctant lorry driver had not told the crew was that not only was there the usual household and farm effects on board, but also some active bee hives. That was why he had been reluctant to go near the lorry to sort it out himself. All in a day's work.

KEITH

IN THE late 1960s the volume of freight moving through Keith cannot be imagined. A typical day started with the midnight freight departure from Aberdeen, which arrived at 2.45a.m. with 40 to 50 wagons. Then the 'Highland Piper' arrived. This was so-called as the wagons were all piped through for vacuum brake, fully fitted and so allowed a faster top speed. This arrived at 3.10a.m. At the Aberdeen end of Keith is a long siding lying parallel to the running lines known as the 'Tattie Road' as potato vans were traditionally stabled there. Wagons to go to Elgin and farther west would be waiting there to be attached to the 'Highland Piper'. The plan was that the engine uncoupled, collected the wagons in the Tattie Road and attached them to the front of the Piper. However, if some of these wagons were not vacuum brake fitted, they would have to be attached to the rear, but before the guard's van. This involved a lot of shunting and general chaos as it interrupted all the other movements going on. The Piper would normally have 70 to 80 wagons and be double-headed from Keith onwards – particularly to provide braking on the descent to Boat O'Brig and the subsequent climb between Keith and Elgin. The Piper would leave Keith at 3.45a.m.-4a.m. if shunting allowed.

This was followed by the 4.30a.m. freight to Elgin. Then the 5.30a.m. freight left to go round to the coast via Carnie Junction. At 5.50a.m. another freight left for Aviemore, via Dufftown and Craigellachie. This train was always full to capacity and drivers would have difficulty pulling away towards Keith Town. They would reverse down the Tattie Road, then open wide the regulator lever to the roof and blast their way through the Dufftown platform of the Junction and take a run at the bank to the Town Station and on up to Speyside.

The short section between Keith Town and Keith Junction was said to be the favourite place for the crews to deposit their bottles of whisky. These would be received at stills for favours, or bartered. As the trains cautiously descended towards the Junction, the bottles would be carefully dropped into the undergrowth. The crews would sign off at the shed and walk home up the road next to the line and recover the bottles without authority knowing.

At 6.20a.m., cattle wagons were dealt with. In between the passenger trains ran to and fro. At 4.55a.m. the Aberdeen to Inverness passenger train arrived with newspapers and parcels for Keith in two BG bogie vans that had to be detached by the Keith shunting loco and crew and shunted into a bay platform for the vital cargo to be uplifted by newsagents and the Post Office in good time. One day, it proved very difficult to detach them. If they were attached to the passenger coaches by screw coupling, the buffers would be in the long position. If coupled using the centre 'Buckeye' coupler, which took the strain, the buffers would be in the short position. This day, the gradient at Aberdeen had been used to assist the attachment of the two vans, which had slammed into each other, coupling the Buckeyes, with the buffers still in the long position. When

The K2 61782 'Loch Eil' at Keith Town.

Standard 4 76106 leaves Keith Town.

uncoupled at Keith (with difficulty – requiring a good squeeze up from the shunting loco) they were drawn back and with squeaking and groaning propelled into the yard. In the dark it was not easy to see the problem, then it became clear. The shunter signalled the driver of the puggie, the two vans were diverted into the loading dock with the granite dead-end and slammed against it. It was lucky that the stiff buffers had not derailed the vans in the curves from Aberdeen.

By now it was 7a.m. and a freight was marshalled and departed to Aberdeen, dodging into loops on the way to keep out of the way of the passenger trains. At 8.45a.m. another freight followed the passenger train to Elgin and at 9.30a.m. another freight set off to go around the coast. At 10.50a.m. another freight set off up Speyside. There was then a short lull, until freights started returning into Keith. At 12p.m. the first Speyside freight ran in with a capacity load of wagons, mostly of whisky casks. At 12.40p.m. another freight set off for Aberdeen. At 2p.m. the coast freight returned, needing its wagons re-marshalling for the destinations. At 4p.m. the next coast freight ran in. At 4.06p.m. a freight was despatched to Aberdeen and another at 6.20p.m. and also at 8.53p.m. Freights departed for Aberdeen taking all sorts of goods (especially whisky) for onward shipment south.

On Tuesdays, always a busy day for whisky, an additional whisky special left for Aberdeen, going direct to Sighthill in Glasgow.

In between all this activity, the empty BGs would be attached to the 12.40p.m. to Aberdeen, next to the engine as they were vacuum braked – requiring a smart shunting move. There were also the local 'trip' workings for the shunting engine and crew. These included at least daily runs out on the main line towards Mulben to deliver wagons and collect full ones from Glentauchers Distillery at Mulben, up the Speyside line with wagons for the siding (still in place today on the Keith Dufftown railway) at Strathmill Distillery and up the truncated Buckie branch to Aultmore Distillery. Because of the gradient the Puggie was permitted to take a maximum of 10 wagons, and they always had to be propelled to Aultmore. This was because if a wagon were to run away, it could not descend to the main line and cause chaos. However, during a storm an empty wagon (erroneously left without the brakes pinned on) was blown away from Aultmore and ran off towards Keith. There are trap points near where the Bond sheds now are, and these derailed the wagon, which ran off and into the River Isla. Recovery of the wagon proved quite a challenge for the Keith recovery crew, but it was relatively unharmed.

With all this activity it is easy to see why the Keith Puggie was employed in three shifts around the clock, shunting wagons and marshalling trains. The ground crew consisted of three men, on three shifts. In between all this, there were the extraordinary (but frequent) events to deal with. For example, the Elgin to Plymouth passenger arrived at Keith with a 'hot box' (overheated axle box due to lack of lubrication) on a coach, which was the seventh on the train of 14 coaches. This necessitated the guard removing the passengers into the other coaches. The shunter squeezed down between the coaches and uncoupled the vacuum pipes, leaving them hanging. This ensured that the train could not move. He then uncoupled the Buckeye couplings and connected the vacuum pipe to

Keith Depot 1955.

the blank coupling plate of the coach in the direction of the engine. The loco then pumped away and rebuilt the vacuum and drew the coaches forward. The remaining coaches' brakes were on. The yard shunter loco then ran smartly forward over the points with the defective coach. The shunter then coupled up the loco and connected the vacuum pipe. He then quickly moved to the rear of the defective coach and broke the vacuum pipe connection hose. Then he uncoupled the coaches and reconnected the vacuum pipe to the blank and signalled with his hand lamp, turning the aspect to green. The shunter driver peeped and drew the defective coach off, through the points and into the dock to await attention from the wagon examiner later.

Meanwhile, the signalman threw the levers and the shunter waved his lamp. The train engine peeped and slowly reversed his coaches back onto the remainder of the train, the driver leaning out to watch the swinging lamp for the distance to the train, he slowed and gradually buffered up, giving just enough pressure to compress the buffers and engage the Buckeye. The shunter now ducked under the buffers and secured the Buckeye, reconnected the vacuum pipes and smartly stepped clear, waving a green aspect on his lamp. The guard watched the vacuum dial climb to 19 inches as the loco pump worked hard. Then he waved a green lamp. The loco peeped again and anxiously started briskly for Aberdeen, trying to make up the lost time. The three men shunting crew quickly reverted to their freight wagon duties as the timetabled freights were arriving and departing and the wagons needed to be in the right order and siding.

It was constant, heavy work in all weathers. The three-man yard crews worked shifts 8a.m. to 4p.m.; 4p.m. to 12a.m.; 12a.m. to 8a.m. One Puggie driver was renowned for being a bit on the cautious side in manoeuvring the loco and wagons and was roundly cursed by a frustrated shunter for being slow. The driver leaned out and retorted that regulations said that locos must move at no more than 10 miles per hour in shunting yards. The exasperated shunter replied: "10 miles an hour! You're just doing 10 miles a day!"

Everything was said in the Doric. Years later, when Newcastle men started a turn to Inverness on HSTs, the locals wondered how the Geordies would get on with an instruction from the signal box to "Just bide fah y're a filey, mun". At its peak Keith had three signal boxes. East, which was incorporated into the station building; West, which controlled the Aultmore branch (the remains of the Highland Railway's Buckie line) and South, which is the one box remaining. This box had 63 levers but today has only 40 with five spare. The boxes were so busy that they had shift working. Keith South had three men, Keith East two men, and Keith West three men. The statistics illustrate the decline. On January 18, 1939 there were 19 through trains, 58 starting and terminating trains, making a total of 77 trains a day, and with specials a four-week average was 79 trains a day. On October 17, 1949 there were 13 through trains, 73 starting and terminating, making a total of 86 while the four-week average was 91 trains a day. By March 1, 1950 there were still 12 through trains, 76 starting and terminating, totalling 88 a day. On January 15, 1989 there were just 14 passenger and two freights a day. Keith Junction had a three-lever ground frame on the platform outside the booking office on the Dufftown platform. Trains entering from Dufftown had to stop by Kynochs Mill and telephone the booking office, who then rang the signal box to gain permission to allow the train into the station. Once received, the levers operated the points and the signal and the train would drift down into the platform. Latterly, it was not required, so the staff grew tomatoes in the little ground frame.

There was a great variety of freight traffic, although whisky predominated and had to receive special attention due to its value. There were full wagons of steel to go to Hamiltons Engineers in Buckie, and always loads of coal for Keith. The freight trains for the coast had to have a guard's van at each end, each van with a fire burning stove, naturally. This was because of the peculiarly restrictive layout at Cairnie Junction. The engine had to run round its train there to take the coast roads and there was not enough room to shunt. The loop could only take 29 wagons and the freight traffic always exceeded this, necessitating the additional trains. The term 'wagon' in this context always referred to a standard wagon length, so a long wagon would be counted at one-and-a-half wagons, a bogie wagon could be counted at two or two-and-a-half wagons.

Other traffic included grain, both inbound malt for the distilleries and outbound wheat and barley, and supplies inbound and special bulbs outbound from the Thorn lighting factory at Buckie which was renowned for employing 365 women.

Lift-on/lift-off containers of prawns kept chilled with dry ice were loaded at Moray Fish at Buckie. Livestock was a regular traffic. Whenever a freight train arrived with livestock wagons they were examined to see if any animals were lying or fallen down. If so, the wagon had to be detached from the train and shunted into the loading dock. The animals would be let out into the pen and any casualties sorted out. They also had access to water on the bank. Cattle usually did not want to go back into the wagon and the yard crew frequently had a hard job with animals, which was a heartily detested traffic causing a lot of difficult work. At one time a cow decided that it most definitely did not want to go back into the wagon and crashed through the sides of the pen and set off for Keith town centre. The crew successfully persuaded the other beasts into the wagon and then retrieved the escapee and, finally, forced it on board. The wagon then had to be attached to the next available train going in the right direction – and there was still the normal work to be done.

Periodically, an embargo would be placed on despatching empty wagons. This was normal when the coal mines went on holiday. They would be held in whichever siding space could be found until the all-clear came through and as many as possible would be added to all freights to clear the yard.

Glenfiddich Distillery received three or four wagons of malt a day. At one time these wagons were embargoed and quickly built up to 50 in the yard, which caused no amount of congestion and double shunting to work round them. For unknown reasons an embargo was put on despatching empty containers on their flat wagons. This went on for some time and it was becoming a real difficulty to find space for wagons. They were shunted up the Aultmore branch, down the Tattie Road and cluttering up the sidings. The siding at Cairnie Junction was filled with 70 to 80 wagons. Then the message came through that a household removal (which was always carried out using door-to-door containers with wadding and packaging which was carefully signed for at each end of the journey) had gone missing. The household furniture and effects were destined for a family who had moved to a house closer to the coast and were rather anxious to have their belongings. Control had traced the movements of the wagon and reckoned it must be at Keith. The weary shunters went in search and checked each of the many containers. They located the furniture in a container that was in the middle of a long line at Cairnie Junction. A lot of careful shunting was needed to extricate the wagon. This took a time as with the volume of trains there were very few periods when the shunter could occupy the running lines and all the sidings were chock full of wagons. A lot of the containers were used on the 'Green Arrow' express freight service which was highly successful and the fore-runner of Freightliner.

The ever-increasing demand for electricity brought the need for transformers. These huge things weighing anything from 90 to 150 tons, arrived on special wagons called, appropriately, 'Transformer Wagons'. They were two bogies connected by two well-shaped beams that supported the transformers. These wagons caused congestion in the yard because Pickfords took a week to get the transformers inched off the wagon and onto their special trailers hauled by mighty Scammell Crusader tractor units which slowly moved them up to the sub-station. There could not have been many Transformer Wagons as there was always a chase on to send them back the moment that they were empty.

Another unusual, but regular vehicle, was the official cinema coach. This arrived tacked onto the rear of a passenger train from Aberdeen. The shunter, smartly drove the 08 diesel shunter out onto the rear of the train. The other shunter had uncoupled the coach from the train and wanted to couple it to the diesel. He threw the link onto the hook and the 08 pulled away sharply. The coach was jerked forward and back as they ran into the headshunt before setting back when the driver turned round to see where he was going to propel the coach. He was most surprised to see a man leaning right out of a window waving his arms furiously. The driver assumed that it must be a passenger from the train who had somehow got through into the cinema coach. He hurriedly propelled the coach into one of the bay platforms and got out. The man turned out to be the cinema attendant who was irate that the rough shunting had shaken up his delicate projection equipment and the coach should have been properly coupled up and carefully shunted. The man had an odd job. He lived in a compartment at the end of the coach and used the facilities at each station that he was sent to on a grand tour of Scotland. The coach had its own generator to provide electricity and was as self-contained as possible. The visit was all planned in advance. The posters had been pasted up around the town announcing the days that the cinema coach would be there and when films would be shown. Despite them being exclusively railway propaganda films, they were very popular. They were good quality films in sound and in colour, and above all they were free. After his allotted time in Keith the attendant and his coach were attached to the next train and sent off to Elgin. This must have been a quite inexpensive, but very effective form of advertising for the railway.

There were seasonal peaks of traffic as well. For some reason Tuesdays were the days when the distilleries despatched the majority of the whisky and the yard would be jammed with wagons. It was not at all unusual for wagons to be left until the next day when capacity would be found on a southbound freight. During the season, potatoes would be despatched, particularly seed potatoes. The vans used for this would spend a long time on the long siding, hence its name Tattie Road. The potatoes could not be handled when it was frosty, so it was a bit unpredictable just when the vans would be required to be shunted into the loading bank road for loading and then immediate despatch. Latterly, seed potatoes were regularly despatched to Portugal. This brought exotic 'Transfesa' wagons registered in both Chiasso, Switzerland and with Italian railways to the North East. One of them developed a fault with an axle and spent many weeks in Elgin yard parked up on sleepers at one end, awaiting the replacement parts.

A freight traffic that was certainly not appreciated locally was train loads of mackerel. When the mackerel were 'running' past Cornwall, they could be scooped up by the thousand. The railway won the job of transporting the fish to Fraserburgh for making into fishmeal. Quite why Keith was unlucky enough to be the receiving yard is not clear. Certainly, the line to Fraserburgh had been closed but it was to Keith that the trains were consigned. The fish were landed at Falmouth into open top mineral wagons, in 25 wagon trains. The train took about three days to reach Keith, by which time the fish smell was unbearable. The shunters drew lots to see who would be unlucky enough to deal with the wagons. The pungent 'bree' was seeping out of the side doors and the wagons were fairly coated in it. The yard mechanical grab was used to transfer the mess to the road lorries. The yard instantly acquired a seagull population, they came from miles away to this free banquet. The Keith men were very happy to despatch the increasingly smelly fish caked wagons away south again. There were two or three such trains that season. The railway received complaints from local residents about the smell, and the yard smelled of fish for years afterwards. The men claim that if you were to dig around the siding, even today, you would release an odour of rotting mackerel.

G. Russell and G. Stewart on the Speyside goods at Craigellachie.

Coal traffic included wagons of open-cast coal mined in the north at Brora, now also a thing of the past. This coal had to be 'tripped'' along to Glentauchers Distillery on the Highland line towards Mulben. Aultmore Distillery also received steady loads of coal, as did Glen Keith Distillery, which consumed seven or eight wagon loads per week. Each wagon could hold 15 tons of coal which had to be transferred into a three ton capacity lorry which shuttled to and fro.

The decline of the freight business was steady and severe, exacerbated by the line closures. The last freight trains to run from Keith to Dufftown, operated by Keith men, are believed to be a Class 25, number 25239, which went up to Dufftown with four wagons of coal. The last train had Class 27, number 27204, which left Keith at 9a.m. on September 1, 1982 with two loaded coal wagons, total 46 tons. The coal was consigned to

Benny Wood of Aberlour, who presumably, unloaded and delivered it from Dufftown yard. The 27 arrived at Dufftown at 9.30a.m. and departed again at 9.45a.m. with four empty coal wagons, total 36 tons. There is no record of bringing those last two wagons back down when they were empty. Perhaps the KDRA have them? It is known that the bridge inspection unit was parked on the viaduct by Dufftown station. This unit had a 'goes-under' arm to allow engineers to be lowered over the side to check the structure. It was there for a week and it is assumed that when it was recovered it brought the two empty wagons down as well. It was an Aberdeen-based crew who worked that last trip.

Keith, at that time, had a big range of shops, including many household names. Boots the Chemist made a claim for a thermos flask that arrived broken. Lipton's claimed for a 1lb. jar of strawberry jam that arrived broken. The stationmaster had to investigate each claim and settle it. He visited the shop, reclaimed the broken jar of jam, paid the claim and buried the broken jar in the yard. All these claims relate to 1937 and purely by chance the claims for that year have survived. A case of 'sherry wine' arrived with one bottle turning out to be just the neck of a bottle in the straw-lined carton. There was no trace of sherry in the box. Obviously, it had been cleverly emptied and replaced with the neck still intact. However, the railway had signed for a full case and had to pay the claim. A soldier had sent his kitbag home to Keith. When he arrived to collect it he found that his army boots had been removed from the kit bag and the thief had substituted his boots – with holes in the sole and completely worn at the heels. A gramophone and records were consigned to a customer in Keith from a shop in Edinburgh. On arrival a record was found on the turntable and scratched – someone had been playing the records on the journey. There were problems with a side of bacon that arrived dirty, and a consignment of flour, part of which was damp. A framed picture arrived with the glass broken. The stationmaster purchased a replacement glass and fitted it to minimise the claim. Hepworth's the tailors claimed for damaged clothing and Balfour Beatty claimed for a missing cable drum. Claims for missing whisky always involved a lot of inquiry. A cask from Aultmore was brought to Keith and transhipped into another wagon to help make up a full load. When the guard checked the train prior to departure he found whisky dripping from the wagon and the Aultmore cask almost empty. The wagon was detached from the train and kept for examination. Sworn statements were taken from everyone concerned – six people. Finally, Customs and Excise were assured that the cask was a 'leaker' and no whisky had been consumed, the claim settled and the wagon released with the other casks still awaiting delivery.

In the days before computers and photocopiers, all such claims entailed masses of paperwork that had to be hand-copied and recorded in books, or duplicated laboriously using purple ink, transfer paper and a press with a wheel to impress the image onto the copy paper.

STATION WORKING

KEITH was such a busy place, and with all this traffic moving night and day, a line had still to be kept clear for the through trains to the Elgin via Dufftown line that did not stop at the Junction. One of these was the mail and newspaper train. The reason why it did not stop at the Junction probably went back to the old rivalry between the Great North of Scotland Railway and the Highland Railway. If the mails were exchanged at Keith the Highland gained the revenue for the section to Elgin on their route via Mulben. The GNSR would stop at Keith Town and then continue via its route to Elgin via Dufftown and Craigellachie and so gain more of the revenue. The railwaymen would catch the 'Subbie' (suburban train – the stopping train) from the Junction and congregate in the booking office at the Town Station awaiting the 'mail' that arrived around 9a.m. No work could be done in the Town offices due to the crowd of railwaymen making tea, making jokes and generally having a good time. Then the mail train would arrive to create a big stir of activity, mail and newspapers taken off, crews changed, parcels off and others on, and depart. Peace would reign and the day to day work of balancing the books would take place. Each ticket (the 'Edmondson' card ones) lived in a compartmented rack in front of the booking clerk. Each ticket had a sequential number. Each clerk had to do his or her 'balance'. This involved noting the number of the next ticket in each little compartment, deducting the number of the ticket that was there when they started duty, multiplying the resultant quantity of each type of ticket (and there were a great many) by the appropriate fare, and the total of all these calculations had to agree with the cash in the till. Plus money from parcels, excess fares, vending machines and less deductions for foreign coins found particularly in the vending machines. The balance was not allowed to be out by even one penny. If there was a shortage after everything had been checked and double checked, the clerk had to dig into his, or her, own pocket to make up the difference. The 'return' of this balance had to be sent to Aberdeen where, no doubt, an array of clerks compiled statistics and more returns from all the many sheets of figures. All this was done without the aid of calculators or computers. It was automatically assumed that everyone could do mental arithmetic. When selling tickets the booking clerks had to add up the amount instantly and give the correct change.

Those trains that did not stop at the Junction created a bit of a challenge to the Keith signalman. They had to exchange single-line tablets with the loco crew while the train was still moving. It would either be powering ahead to overcome the gradient up to the Town station, or be running away down the gradient to carry on to Aberdeen. In either case they were often travelling faster than the regulation speed. One day, the signalman was standing bravely on the sleepers in front of the signal box watching with trepidation the diesel-powered train thundering down towards him. The second man was leaning right out of his window; the signalman held

Class D42 at Elgin June 1942. Tender cab for branch work.

The signalman walks back to the signal box with the token over his shoulder, at Drummuir, 21.10.54.

Signalman Charlie Grant at Dufftown on the last day of passenger trains.

Mortlach Distillery and sidings at Dufftown.

out the token and looked to hook up the offered token. The hoop was snatched out of his hand with such speed that it pulled his wedding ring off his finger. Fortunately, the ring broke, otherwise he would have lost his finger. His finger and hand swelled up and took a long time to return to normal. His wedding ring was jammed into the buckle of the leather pouch and he got it back, but has never worn his wedding ring since.

Everything came and went by train. A prize bull was bought in the south and arrived at Ballindalloch consigned to a Mr. Grant in Glenrinnes, who would come to collect. The bull did not appreciate the journey in the cattle wagon and was stamping and kicking and making a din when it was shunted into the dock. With great trepidation the porter opened the wagon door and jumped for his life as the bull charged out and galloped off down the line towards Craigellachie. Signal box contacted signal box all down the line to alert crews of the charging bull, and if seen to report its whereabouts. It was located, tired, but happy, in a field next to the line and was successfully rounded up and delivered to a relieved Mr. Grant.

At Longmorn, a curious locomotive built by Aveling and Porter, based on their successful traction engine design but fitted with railway wheels, operated the three stills of Longmorn, Benriach and Glenlossie, the latter one-and-a-half-miles away. This loco was replaced with a diesel locomotive which has survived. The 'branch' to Glenlossie closed before the railway proper between Rothes and Elgin closed, but the train, still running on GNSR track, continued in operation running between the two stills until February 29, 1980. The loco and wagons were donated to the Strathspey Railway.

Dufftown, with its seven distilleries, was an important source of traffic. One of the distilleries, Mortlach, is very old being opened in 1823 and is close to an ancient church that is said to have been founded there in 450 BC. The GNSR built a branch line to tap into traffic there. Just to the Keith side of the viaduct over the River Fiddich beyond Dufftown Station is a lime works. On October 5, 1891 a branch was opened to 'Parkbeg' lime works, subsequently known at Parkmore Lime Works Siding. In 1900 this was extended along to Glendullan Distillery and onwards crossing the Huntly road by a level crossing and continuing to Mortlach. The procedure was for the train to arrive from Keith and collect the token from Dufftown signal box. Then it reversed back across the viaduct, used the token to operate the ground frame and head into the branch. If another train was due to pass on the main line, or if the shunting took longer than expected, someone would be despatched from Dufftown Station to recover the token, effectively locking the freight train on the branch. Then, when it wanted to come out again, the fireman would have to walk to the station to collect the token again. The branch as far as Mortlach was closed on March 23,1964 and from Glendullan and Parkmore from November 7, 1966.

The distilleries created the majority of the goods traffic, but there were also other sidings opened for any other source of traffic that was

Driver G. Russell at the Aberlour yard.

available. A siding was built to the Morayshire Brick and Tile works on the Lossiemouth line out of Elgin. Timber sidings were laid down at Knockando in 1918, but it is not known when they were lifted. Apart from the lime works at Dufftown, there was another one which was given a siding on June 1, 1863 and known as Drummuir Lime Kiln Sidings. By 1884 it was known as Botriphine and was closed in 1890. However, it was reopened in 1894 and on January 1, 1898 it was renamed Towiemore. It was only from around 1924 that passengers were carried from the little halt and it did not appear on the public timetable until 1937. Right up to the 1980s the station 'building' was the original – a short GNSR coach body! It was bought by a local farmer and taken away for use as a hen house.

It is incredible to believe that all this infrastructure, employment and way of life has gone in such a short space of time. It is important to record all these full of life details that are still within living memory for future generations to understand the way it was.

Ron Smith and the Keith & Dufftown Railway Association would like to acknowledge and thank the following people for the use of their photographs in the making of this book:

Charles Mitchell Page 2.

Roy Hamilton Pages 3, 8, 10, 41.

Douglas Hume Pages 6, 26 (top), 50 (both).

The Charlie Jamieson Collection Pages 23 (both), 47 (both), 56, 62 the front & rear covers..

Douglas Gray Pages 26 (lower), 27 (both), 30 (both).

Hamish Stevenson Page 59 (middle & lower).

John Low Page 38.

James Currie (Mike MacDonald Photographs) Page 25 (lower).

Hugh Davies (Photos of the Fifties) Page 9.

Charles Beaton / GNOSRA, Page iii

J.Hay collection / the late J.Keir, Page 1, page 5, page 19 (both) page 20 (both)

H.Duncan Page 12 (both) page 51, page 59 (upper) and pages 44 and 45 tickets.

The late J.Keir, Pages 14,15, (all) and page 25 upper.

The late R. Gault, Pages 17, 35,37, 40

John Anderson, Page 60.